The Places
of
Marguerite Duras

THE PLACES OF MARGUERITE DURAS
Marguerite Duras and Michelle Porte

Originally published by Les Éditions de Minuit, 1977
This edition published by Magic Hour Press, 2025

Edited and designed by Jordan Weitzman
Translated by Alison Strayer
Proofread by Charity Coleman

Images and text © Les Éditions de Minuit, 1977
This edition © Magic Hour Press, 2025
Introduction © Durga Chew-Bose, 2025

The publisher would like to thank Georges Borchardt,
Pauline Cochran, Moyra Davey, Jason Fulford, Craig
Garrett, Thomas Simonnet, Francis Schichtel

Printed in Italy by EBS

Distributed by
ARTBOOK/DAP
75 Broad Street, Suite 630
New York, NY 10004
Artbook.com

ISBN 978-1-7389013-5-7

www.magichour.press

Marguerite Duras
Michelle Porte
Translated by Alison Strayer

The Places
of
Marguerite Duras

Magic Hour Press
2025

Introduction
Durga Chew-Bose

Two winters ago, I was travelling from Paris to Marseille by train, on my way to scout the villa that would eventually become my film's primary location. We were a small group which included my producers, our cinematographer, and our production designer. Our scout, Mathilde, was waiting for us at Gare de Marseille-Saint Charles, and from there, we would pile into her van and head east, curving the clifftop Route des Crêtes and its panoramic views of the Mediterranean coastline.

Two winters ago, is too recent for nostalgia but sufficiently distant to warrant some romance, and so, I remember that time with affection and practical details. I packed sweaters, pens, a notepad. I thought a deck of playing cards would prove useful, and it did. It took a couple of games for everyone to acquaint themselves with rules they'd long forgotten, like the difference between a set and a run or if an ace can wrap around and follow a king. It can't.

As for books, I only brought one, Marguerite Duras's *Les Lieux*, partly for its topicality and mostly because I believe in the talismanic properties of carrying books whose words provide counsel no matter what page flips open; an intelligence not necessarily for what is needed in the moment, but for what can specify purpose and intuit future patterns. After all, I was on a film scout, and *Les Lieux* was compiled from interviews between Michelle Porte and Duras, in which the writer and filmmaker expounds (in her meditative, inward yet direct manner) on the places, locations, and homes that formed "instant attachment," pressing her to make films and consider the potency of her past. These places acted as both accomplice and muse—too consuming to merely pass off as other characters in her films, more similar perhaps to a syndrome; a presence Duras could not ignore.

These places lodged themselves in Duras's imagination with prodigious, incantational force. Like the crumbling Château Rothschild in Boulogne, where her Calcutta-set *India Song* was shot, or how the transposable nature of the house in *Nathalie Granger* (shot in Neauphle-le-Château), meant the location and the film became somehow indistinguishable forms. Is it a film? Or is it house? Or is it a film-shaped house? And which came first? The house or the story? Or the women who live in this house, who are the thrumming centre of the house, and who bring it to life by testifying to its portrayal of time passing, like daylight waning or flies dying inside of lamp-shades. According to Duras, both examples are cinema, which I'd venture is different than calling something cinematic.

Duras's regard for her locations was dogged. The vision—"the urge to film," she calls it—hinged on the setting, the garden, the doorway, the walls and objects, the chest of drawers, the cobwebs in the dining room, the little kitchen at the end of the hall. "I'd have sooner given up on the film than to give up that location," she says of Château Rothschild. But it's more than that. It's always more than the cover of willful terms. The urgent spark of connection that Duras speaks of, at least in terms of *India Song*, "cannot be explained simply in terms of having found a place to shoot a film of fiction. Something else was speaking through it," she says. It was a place with allegorical powers where she could "talk about the end of the world." The location was not a place but an awareness, suitable for story and poised for the pureness of disaster.

The first villa we saw was in the small fishing port of Cassis, a thirty-minute drive from Marseille. Designed by the architect Fernand Pouillon, villa Barthélémy's simple shapes and natural dialogue between the sun and midday shadows, the sea and the swimming pool, were instantaneous. I belonged to this villa. Even its smaller parts, like a serving hatch in the kitchen or the patios built to accommodate the pines, specified something beyond my control. We saw other villas afterwards, but it was mostly out of courtesy. She was the one! Like Duras, the villa provided me with an urge to film. Five months later we began production and still—a year and a half since wrapping our principal photography, with the movie's release nearing—the vibrancy of villa Barthélémy has not run out. It has left an aftertaste, something resembling desire. As Duras notes, hers are works of ongoing rise. "I get the feeling that my films begin the day after they've been seen." They begin, only to begin again, "from that place of passion" that outlives art as merely a form of leisure. Her house was a film. Her films are a house. A place you go to live.

This book was compiled by Michelle Porte from interviews for the two tevision broadcasts entitled Les Lieux de Marguerite Duras, *produced by the Institut national de l'audiovisuel, and aired in May 1976 on TF1.*

1

Marguerite Duras :
I could talk for hours about this house, about the garden. I know every part of it—where all the old doors were, everything, the walls of the pond, all the plants, where all the plants are, even the wild plants, everything.

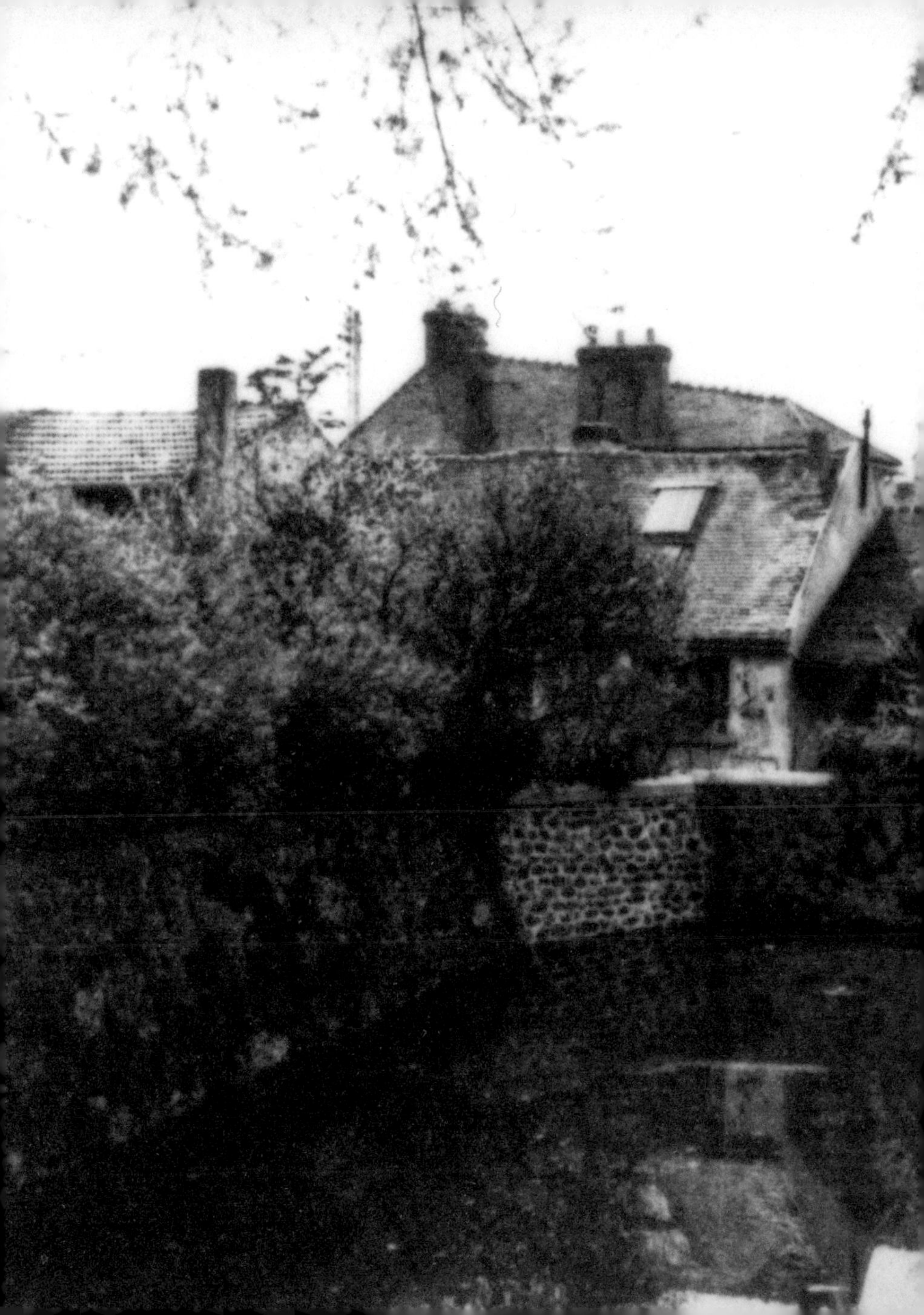

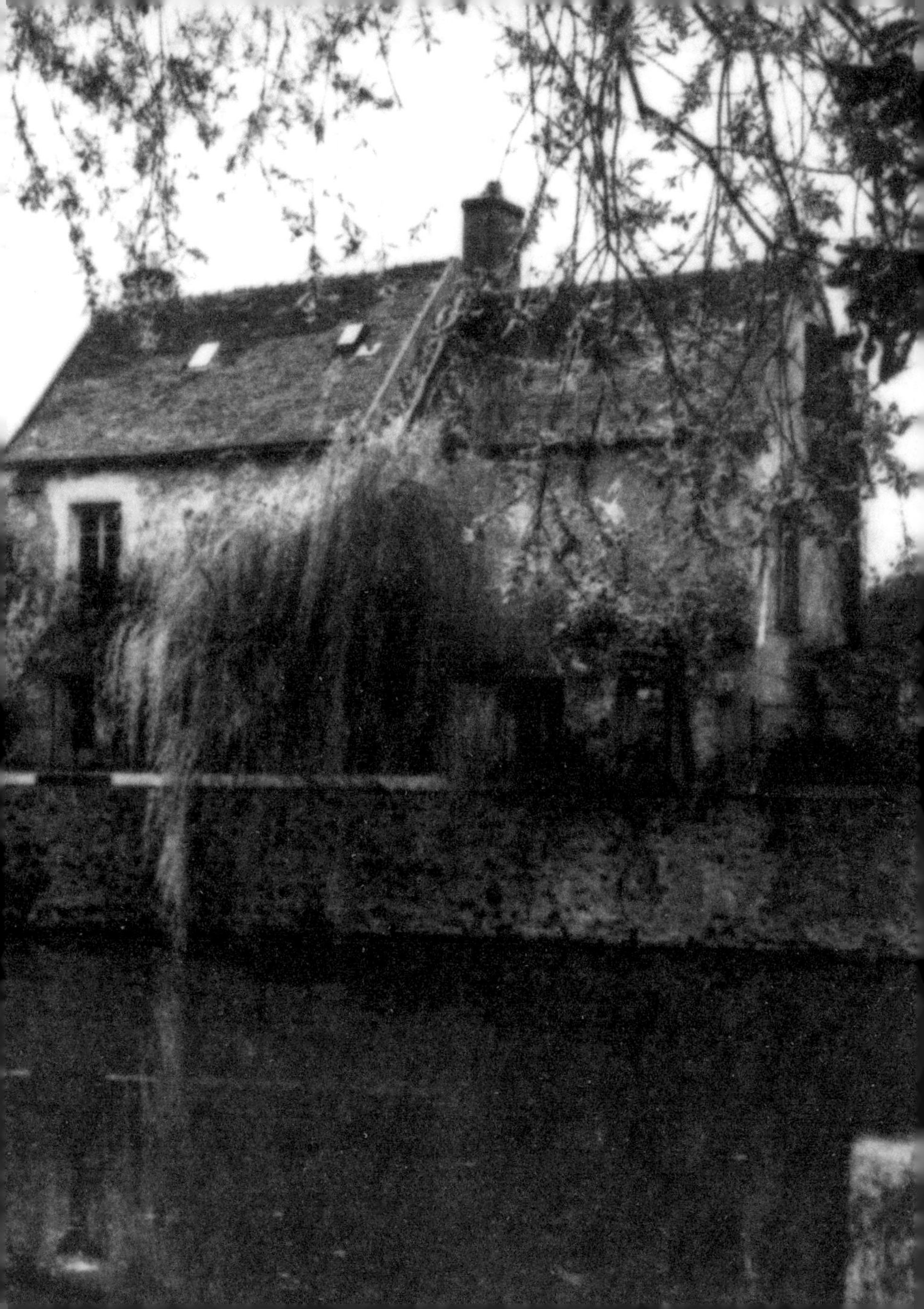

Je fais des films pour occuper
mon temps. Si j'avais la force
de ne rien faire je ne ferais rien
C'est parce que je n'ai pas la force
de ne m'occuper à rien que je fais
des films. Pour aucune autre raison
C'est là le plus vrai de tout ce
que je peux dire sur mon entreprise
Duras

Michelle Porte :

Marguerite Duras, you once wrote: "I make films to fill my time. If I had the strength to do nothing, I would do nothing. It is only because I haven't the strength to do nothing that I make films. For no other reason. That is the truest thing that I can say about my practice.

M. D. :

That is true.

M. P. :

Would you also say: It's because I haven't the strength to do nothing that I write books?

M. D. :

When I was writing books, I don't think I was there yet, no… I only reached that point when I stopped writing books, practically. I mean when I stopped writing every day and started making films. Except that when I stopped writing, I stopped doing something that was… well, the most important thing that had ever happened to me, by which I mean writing. But I no longer know what my reasons were for writing in the first place. Maybe they overlap with the others. What amazes me is that not everyone writes. I have a secret admiration for people who don't write, and also, of course, for people who don't make films.

M. P. :

Many of your films take place in a house that is cut off from the outside world.

M. D. :

Here, yes, in this house. Every time I'm here, every time, I feel the urge to film. There are places like that, which make you want to film. I would never have believed that a place could have that kind of power, that strength. All the women in my books have lived in this house, all of them. It is only women who inhabit places, not men. This house was inhabited by Lol V. Stein, by Anne-Marie Stretter, by Isabelle Granger, by Nathalie Granger—all kinds of other women too. Sometimes when I enter the house, I feel a profusion of women, just like that. It's been inhabited by me, too, completely. I think it's the place in the world that I've inhabited the most. And when I talk about these other women, I believe that these other women contain me too. It's as if we were endowed with a kind of permeability. The time in which they are immersed is a time before words, before men. A man, when he cannot name things, is lost; he's in a state of adversity, he is disoriented. Men have a talking sickness, women do not. All the women I see here are silent at first. I don't know what will happen later, but to begin with, they are silent for a long time. They are embedded in the room, as if they were part of the walls and the objects in the room.

When I'm in that room, I have no sense of disturbing its inherent order, as if the room itself, or rather the place, hadn't noticed that I was there, that a woman was there. She already had a place in the room. I'm probably talking about the silence of the place.

Michelet says that witches came into being just like that. During the Middle Ages, the men were away at the war of the seigneur or the Crusades, and the women remained in the countryside completely alone, isolated for months on end, in the forest, in their huts, and that was how, in solitude—a kind of solitude we can't imagine now—they started talking to trees, to plants, to wild animals. In other words, they entered into... how shall I put it? They invented, reinvented, a kind of intelligence with Nature. They returned to an intelligence that must have dated back to prehistoric times, if you will.

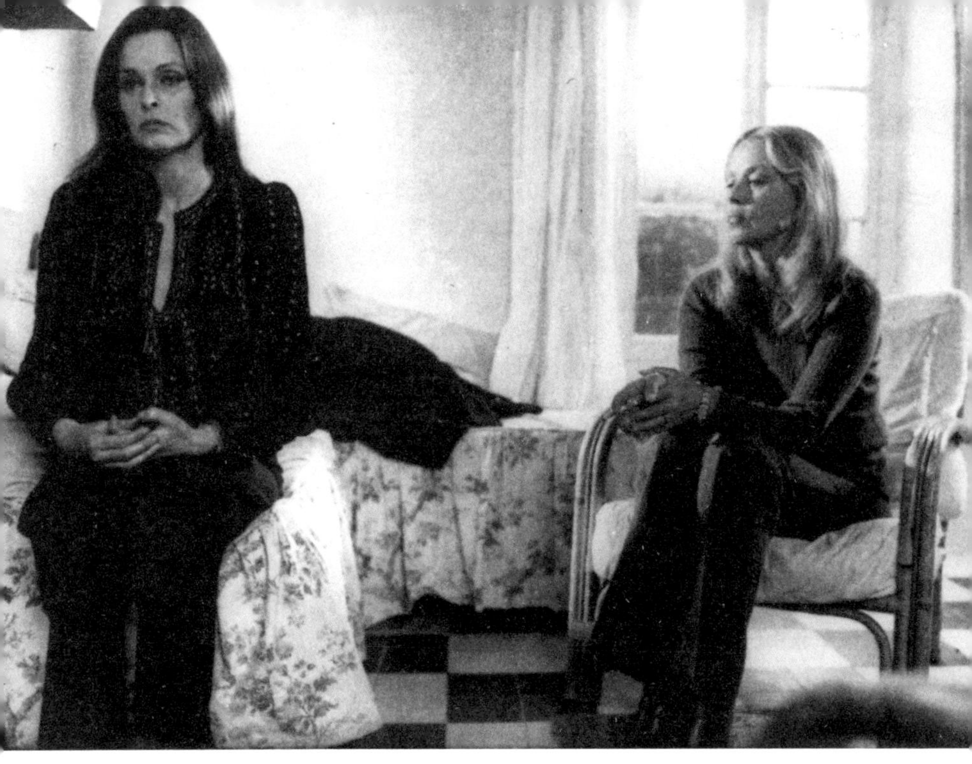

And they were called witches, and they were burned. It is said that there were a million of them, starting from the Middle Ages, up to the beginning of the Renaissance. Women were burned, up until the seventeenth century.

Are the women in your films and books—I'm thinking of the woman in *Nathalie Granger*, I mean Isabelle Granger, and Élisabeth Alione in *Détruire, dit-elle,* and Véra Baxter, in *Baxter, Vera Baxter*—aren't they too the witches of Michelet, in a sense?

M. D. :

Things haven't changed for us women. We're still at the same point... yes. Things are still the same. They haven't really moved at all. Me, I have a kind of relationship with this house and this garden that men will never have with a habitat, a place.

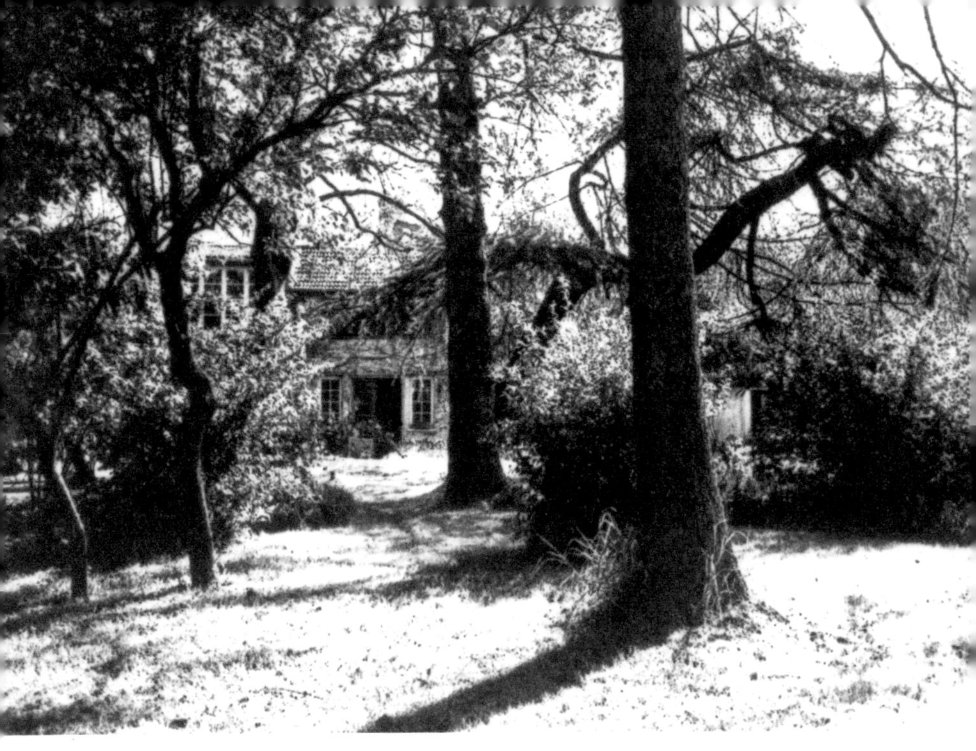

This enclosed perimeter formed by the house, the park, and the forest appears in almost all your films.

M. D. :

Yes, the forest is connected to the park. The park is the beginning of the forest. The park announces the forest. There is a park in *Détruire*. There is a park in *India Song*, in *Nathalie Granger*. In *Jaune le soleil*, there's a black park where the dogs of the Jews are. The forest is the forbidden. I mean that I don't know exactly what the forest is in *Jaune le soleil*; I call it the forest of nomadism, the forest of the Jews. I don't know what the link is between that forest and the forest in *Détruire*, which people are afraid of, which a certain part of the bourgeoisie is afraid of, which men are afraid of and which they massacre. As for us, we become part of the forest, we insert ourselves into it, you see. Men go there to hunt, to punish and to monitor.

M. P. :

When speaking of the film *Nathalie Granger*, you once said: "What I see before anything else in *Nathalie Granger*, before the film, is the house."

M. D. :

Yes. Perhaps it was by dint of being here so much that the house came to seem like a container to me. Anyway, it's a vision I'm expressing here, not an idea. Houses can be seen as places where people come for refuge, where they come to seek reassurance. But I think that the house is also a place that is closed to something else. Yes, there's something else going on there besides all the usual things related to security, reassurance, family, home sweet home, etc. There is also a horror of the family that is deeply ingrained in every house, the need to escape, all the suicidal moods. It all goes together. It is strange, people usually go home to die. They prefer to die at home. The moment a person goes into a certain kind of slump, they want to go home. The house is a mysterious place and… I don't know if people in cities today really know what it is. I discovered what it was with this house. Though I did have a house once, in the Dordogne, when I was six, which my mother sold… I should tell you that I was the daughter of a public servant… and that throughout my childhood, all I did was move from place to place. When my parents

changed jobs, I changed houses. And after that, I rented flats in
Paris, and this is the first time I've had a house of my own. And...
it's a little as if I'd been born here; I've made it so much my own
that I feel it has belonged to me since... since before I was born.

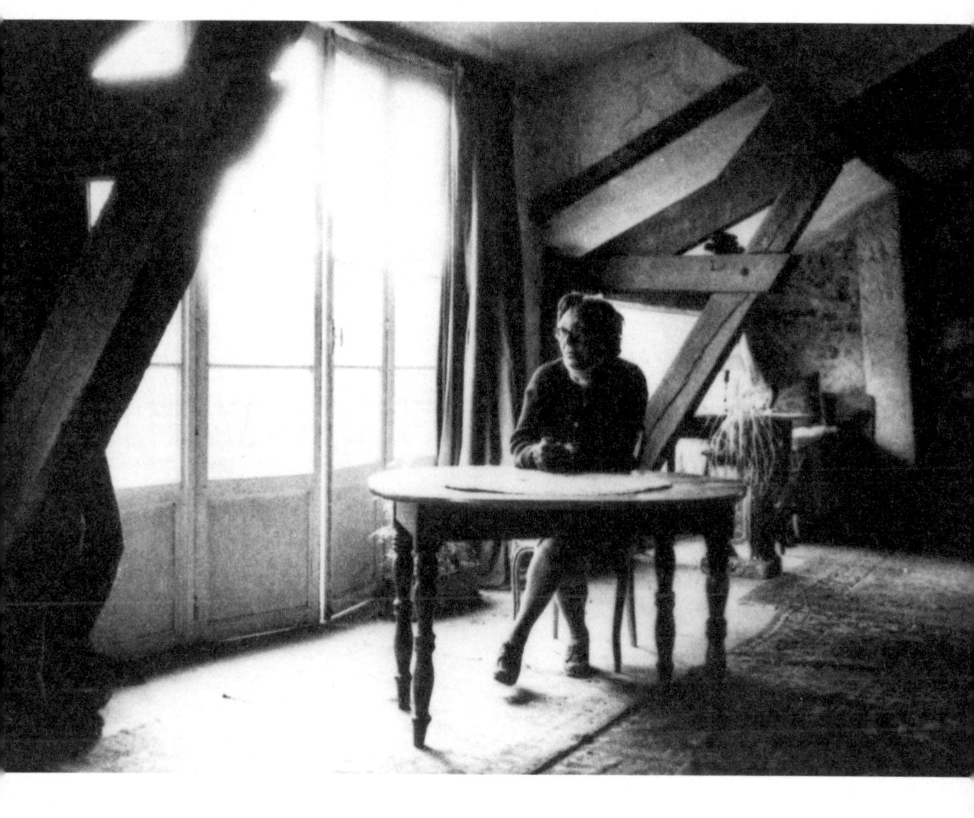

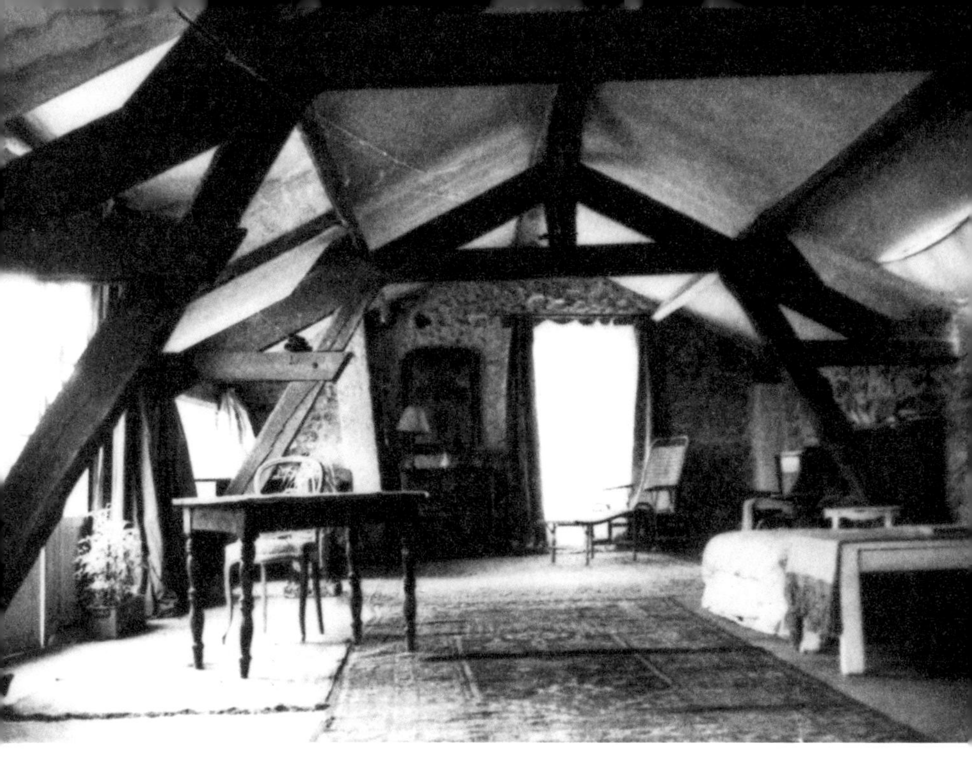

This part of the house used to be a barn. I have searched but found no trace of writing, or of anyone passing through here. I was very struck by this. No photos, no inscriptions, no books, no letters, nothing. There's a date on the wall of the pond. I think it's 1875. But you find things in the ground. We found keys and knives, penknives, you know, bits of crockery. Buried in the ground, very deeply. There are two centuries of household rubbish down there. Bits of toys, bits of marbles, whole marbles too. But in the house itself, nothing.

M. P. :

When you talk about Isabelle Granger, you say: "She is wandering like a prisoner."

M. D. :

Yes, I see Isabelle Granger as a prisoner of the house, a prisoner of herself, of her life, if you like, and of a sort of infernal circuit that ferries her from the love of her children to her conjugal duties, as they say, and I think that it's the whole substance of her life that is contained here. It's as if, as she wanders through the house, she were walking around herself, going around her own body. Isabelle Granger seems to me to inhabit the house entirely, as if the house itself had a woman's shape and she were filling every part of it, if you like. That is how strongly I feel the unity between this woman and her home. But that is not an accident. If I am saying this, it is probably because I've felt the same thing myself. And if I'm compelled to put women and nothing but women in this house all the time, that is not an accident either. For me this place is a place of women.

M. P. :

And you think that only a woman can inhabit a place so completely?

M. D. :

Yes, only a woman can be at ease there, can adhere to a place completely, yes, without getting bored. I don't think I ever walk through this house without looking at it. And I think that this gaze is a woman's gaze. A man returns to the house in the evening; he eats there, sleeps there, warms himself there, and so on. A woman is different. There's a kind of ecstatic gaze, the gaze of a woman looking at the house from inside herself, at her home and all the objects, which are obviously the container of her life, and even, for most women, a *raison d'être*, almost, that men cannot share. I say at one point, when Isabelle Granger walks in the park, this park, that we don't wonder at the fact of her walking there. Isabelle Granger is in the park instead of being somewhere else, in a bedroom, for example. Instead of being somewhere else, she is there. She is walking very slowly in the park, and it seems completely natural. If a man did that, if a man walked through the park at the same pace, with the same calm and tranquillity, people would not believe it. They'd say, he is deep in thought because he is going through a rough patch. They'd say, he is pacing up and down in the park. No one would say he's walking in the park. They'd say, he's gone there to think. And the women in the houses would worry to see a man in that state, in the park, prey to his thoughts, as people used to say. In *Nathalie Granger*, this house is really a place of women, a house of women. Moreover, that's the way it always is because a house is made by women. It's exactly the same as with the proletarian. The proletarian's work belongs to him, to the proletarian. The proletarian's tools *are* the proletarian. In a similar way, the house belongs to the woman; the woman is a proletariat, as you know, a thousand years old. And the house belongs to her just as as the proletarian's tools of labour belong to the proletarian.

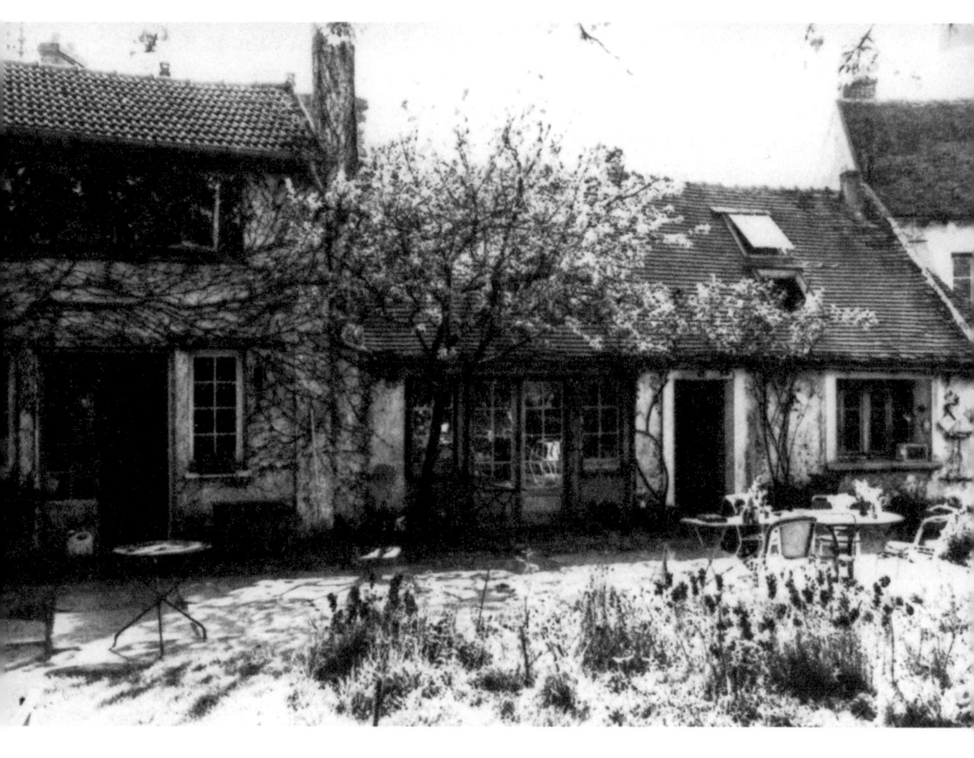

M. D. :

Yes, the fact that the woman is herself a home, the baby's home, and has that sense of protecting the child with her body, of encircling the baby with her body, cannot be unrelated to the way in which she is herself embedded in the habitat, in her home. That's for sure.

I think there's essential difference between a woman who's had a child and a woman who hasn't had a child. I see childbirth as a guilty act. It's as if one were casting the child away, abandoning him. The closest thing to murder that I've ever seen is childbirth. The ejection of a sleeping child. It is life itself that is sleeping, that is completely asleep in a state of extraordinary bliss, and waking up. Perhaps it's a part of the experience of motherhood. I don't think we know very much about it. There is a lot of hearsay out there, and we're mired in prejudice. It's true that it is murder. The baby is like a being in a state of bliss. The first sign of life is a scream of pain. You know, when the air first enters the alveoli in the baby's lungs, it causes unspeakable suffering. The first sign of life is pain.

M. P. :

The scream.

M. D. :

It's more than a scream, you know. These are the cries of slaughter, of someone being killed, being murdered, of someone screaming no.

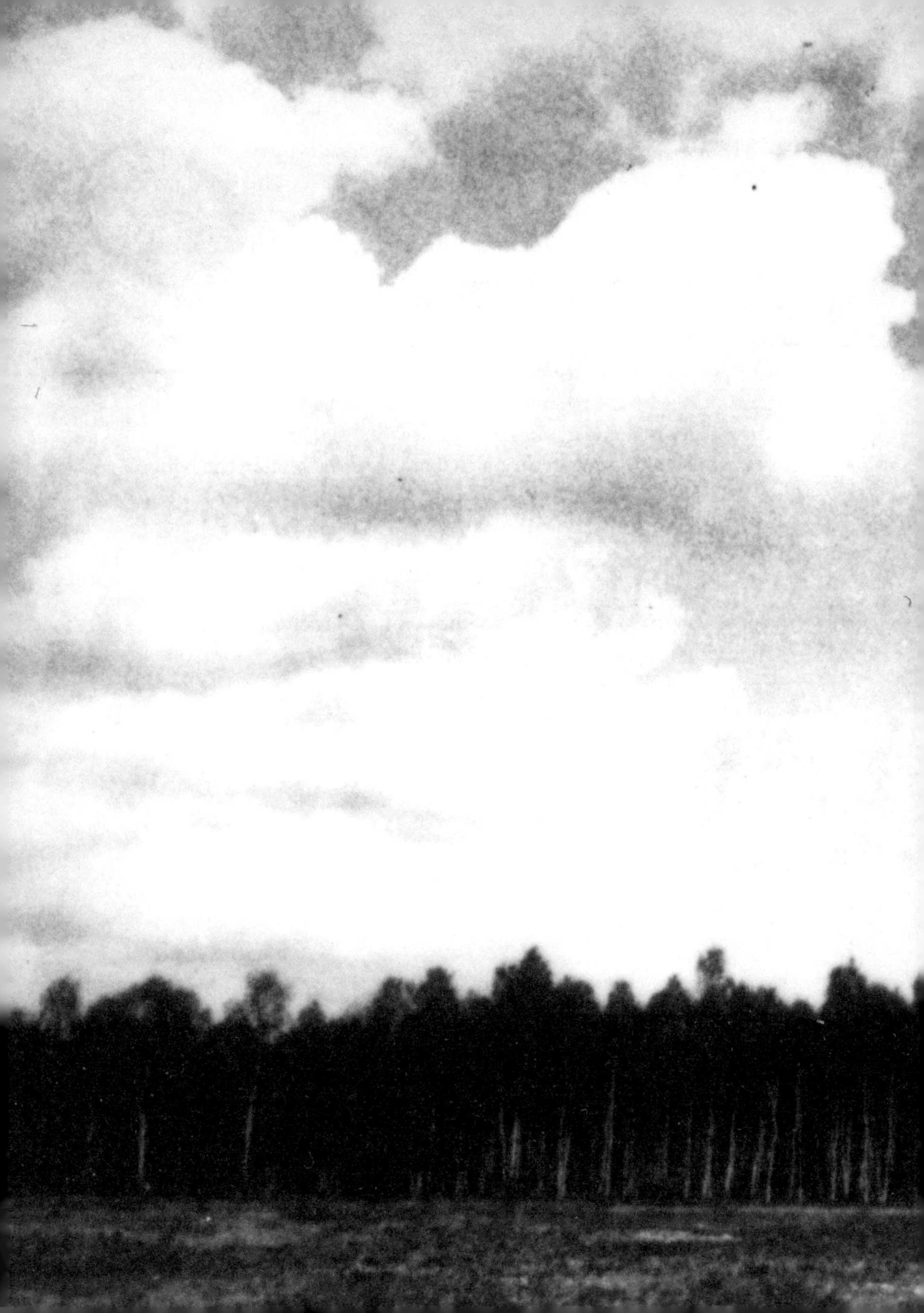

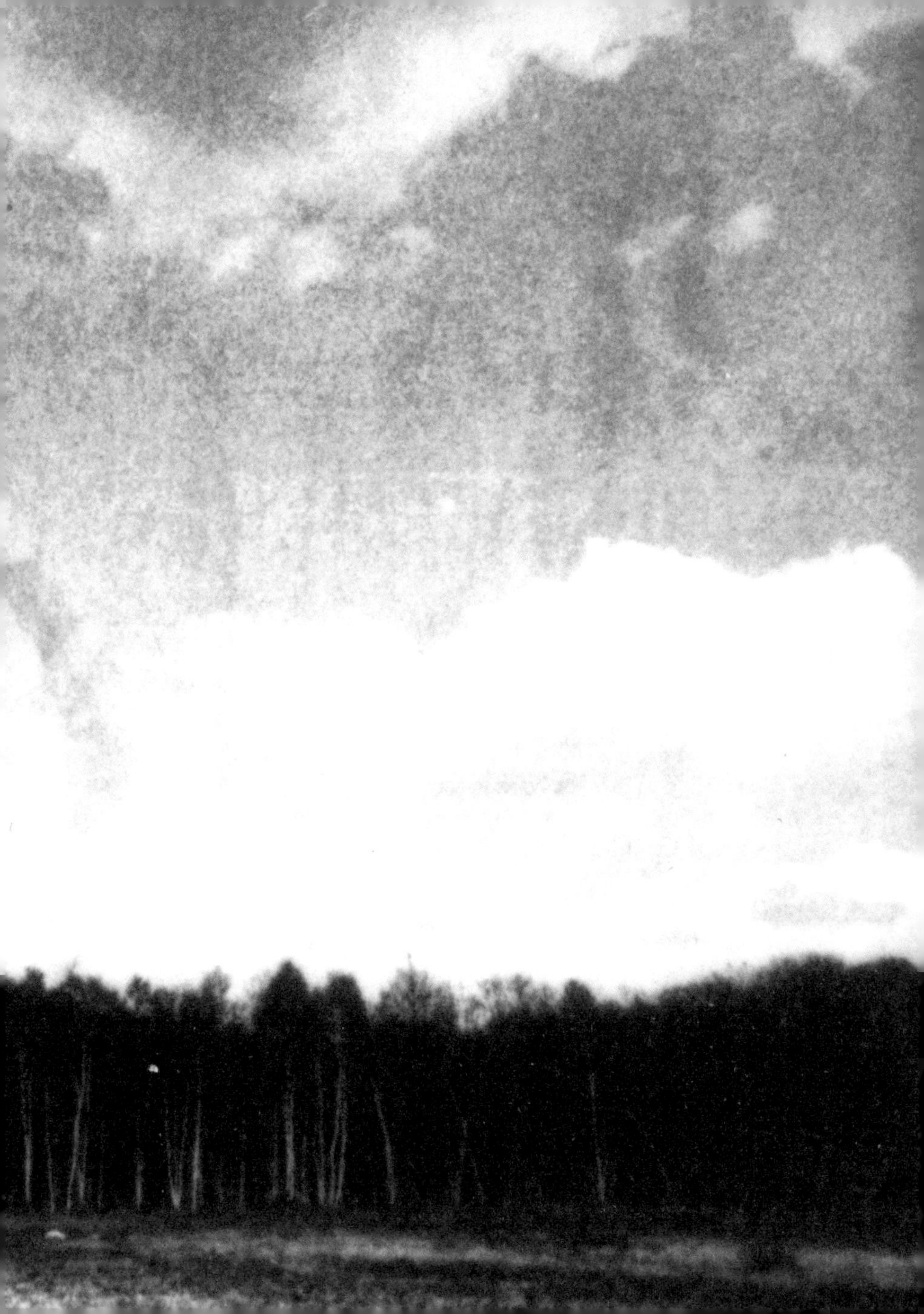

M. P. :

In *Nathalie Granger,* when the outside gets inside the house, it's extremely violent. It's the voice of the radio, the crime of the Yvelines, the manhunt in the forest of Dreux.

M. D. :

Violence inhabits the forest. In *Détruire*, the forest is supposed to be inhabited by violence. When Alissa and Stein go off to love each other, it's to the forest that they go.

M. P. :

They do. But...

M. D. :

The others, no. The others look at the forest, they look at it from a distance but they don't go into it. The forest is the forest of my childhood. I know it is. When I was very little, a child in Indochina, I lived on land near virgin forest, and the forest was forbidden because it was dangerous; there were snakes, insects, tigers and all that. But we children went in there anyway. We weren't afraid. We were born there, we weren't afraid of the forest. But my mother, who was from the north, who was European, was afraid of the forest. She was from the north of the world, my mother. In fact she wasn't afraid of the forest, she was afraid of the strangeness of the tropics, which she'd discovered late in life. And we children swarmed about in the forest like everything else that lived there. My little brother and I were completely at home there, in *Barrage contre le Pacifique.* We ate the fruits of the forest, we killed animals, we walked barefoot on the trails, we swam in the little rivers, we hunted crocodiles. He was twelve, I was going on nine. When we were supposed to be napping, we'd run away, and quite naturally, we ran towards danger. It was only later that I felt afraid of the things we used to do. The forest belongs to madmen, you understand? And in my life, the forest belonged to childhood. The forest where I went as a child was full of children who were disobeying just like us. And in the back countries of *Barrage contre le Pacifique* beggars came at night to bed down in clusters of hanging vines. They built fires, they slept there; and, when I talk about the nomadism of the Jews in *Jaune le soleil*, you know, about those burned-out fires everywhere, I think there's a link with what I lived as a child.

It's the forest of journeys, if you like, real journeys. And that is childhood too, you see. Yes. But not everyone in my books is afraid of the forest. The children of Dreux take refuge there. The little sixteen-year-old murderers from the Yvelines take refuge in the forest. The forest becomes dangerous because of them. People are afraid of the forest, just as they are afraid of those young thugs, as of all kinds of violence. But now I'm afraid of the forest. I never go into a forest alone. It's a place, an… I don't know, an unsettling place, a very, very ancient place; and in theory, all forests date back to prehistoric times. They're haunted places in a sense—I do not reject the word.

M. P. :

As if the forest were a sacred place, in the ancient meaning of the word?

M. D. :

Yes, you know, it was to the forest that we women, the first women, started speaking freely, in a language we'd invented. As I said earlier about Michelet and how women started talking to animals and plants, it was a language of their own they spoke, not one that they had learned. It was because of that free speech that women started to abandon their duties

to men, and indeed to their homes. It's the voice of freedom,
but naturally it frightens people.

M. P. :
Yes.

M. D. :
Completely.

[*The cries of children from outside.*]

M. D. :
School is letting out. You can hear them from one end of the
house to the other. The house is long and narrow. Winter and
summer, you hear the kids go by. I hear them in the middle of
winter, it's eight in the morning, eight-thirty, the middle of the
night, and they're playing.

The forest and music are somehow connected. When I'm
afraid of the forest, of course, it's myself I'm afraid of. You see,
I've been afraid of myself since puberty, haven't I? Before puberty,
I wasn't afraid in the forest.

Music terrifies me too. I think that in music there's a kind of
completion, a time we cannot grasp now in the present. There is,

in music, an annunciation of a time in the future when we'll be able to hear it. Music… well, it overwhelms me, I cannot listen to it, though I could when I was young; when I was still ignorant and naive, I could listen to music. Now it's very difficult for me to listen to music without being… well… overwhelmed… Of course, we can't talk about music, I can't talk to you about music. Someday I'll no longer be afraid of it. For the time being, it is frightening, as the future is frightening. I think that people like Bach, for example… Bach lacked understanding of his own music. Sometimes I compare him to Goya. Goya's extraordinary pictorial intelligence could only be coupled with a kind of imbecility when it came to daily life. I can't imagine Goya being any other way. What's more, his life is proof of what I've just said. He was a flatterer, he had completely naive illusions—or anyway, he behaved like a little boy all his life. You cannot see in the way he did unless you're somehow impervious. You cannot *see* with that kind of acuity except if that acuity has no repercussions. Otherwise, you would die. Bach would have died if he'd been aware of what he was doing. Besides, you know, he didn't say a single thing worth noting in all his life. Nor did Goya.

Of everything I've done, all the films I've made, the shot that moves me the most is the one of music, the musical notations, the sheet music in *Nathalie Granger*. We put a mass of sheet music on the floor. The camera pans across the scores and, I think, finishes on the cover of *The Art of the Fugue*. It must have moved very close to the *Chaconne*, and ended on the hardest piece, the *Art of the Fugue*, or perhaps the *Goldberg Variations*, I don't know, while the child is playing scales. And, if you like, the distance that must be covered between the scales of the child—the scales of childhood, or of the childhood of man, or the childhood of humanity—and that language we cannot decipher, the language of music, that distance overwhelms me. In *Jaune le soleil*, I compare Bach to the proletariat. I said, here there is a mountain of cement, and over there a mountain of music… nobody understood… *(Laughs)* I'll explain it now. Between the mountain of cement, the cement transported and worked on by the proletariat, and the mountain of music, I see an equivalence of labour. Over the two mountains, of cement and of music, the same darkness reigns. I was almost going to say the same deafness.

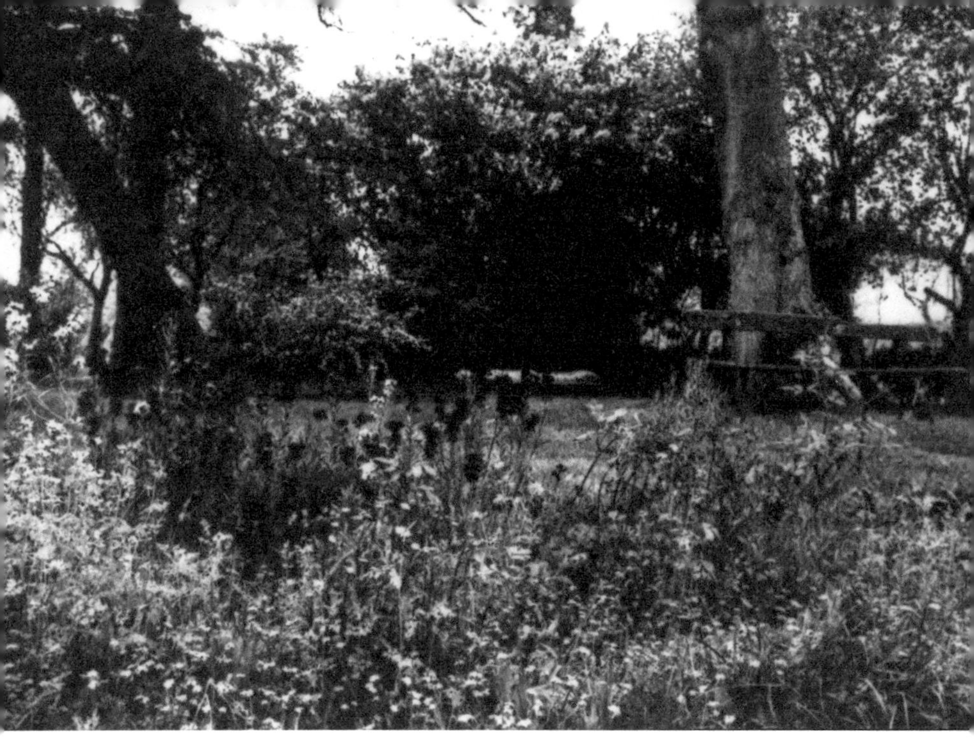

I wrote a page not long ago in which I talked about the humidity of the park, the park that was streaming with moisture, and so on. And then I reread the text and saw that I'd used the plural. I'd written "the humidities of the park," whereas I'd thought "the humidity of the park." Of course I left the plural. It was a slip of the hand. But it was so much more accurate, considering the park's multiplicity, all its species, to talk about humidities—the humidity of the earth, the humidity of the trees, the humidity of the fruit, of the water, the air, etc. The plural was required.

In short, you set out mistrusting yourself, you set out to write with a sense of guilt and second-rate baggage that others have thrown together for you. You don't set out in a state of freedom. You must have faith in yourself. You have faith in others… you have faith in love… you have faith in desire… but then, in relation to yourself, you're full of mistrust. Why? It's not right. I trust myself as I would trust another. I trust myself completely.

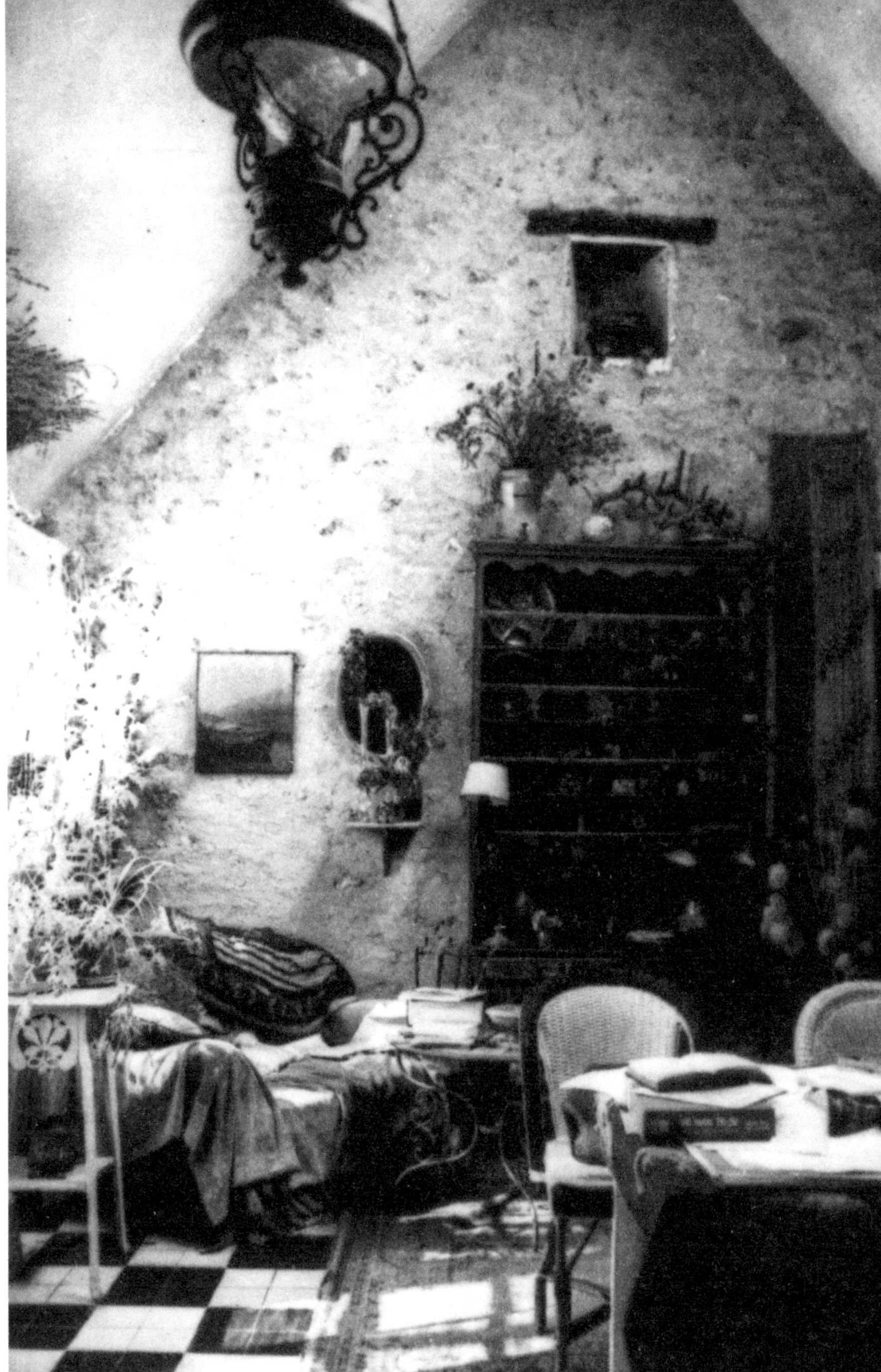

M. D. :

This is my favourite room in the house, perhaps because of the high ceilings, I don't know. But I've never written, never worked in this room. It's a communal room, especially in the summer, when everyone is here.

There are still swallows' nests in the corners of the big beams, there. The swallows fled when we moved into the room. We couldn't get them to stay.

Have you seen the cobwebs, there, in the dining room? What can one do, I've never found a stick long enough to reach all the way to the top, so we leave them there. You get used to them. That's another prejudice—about cobwebs. They're actually quite beautiful in a certain light.

Every summer we cut the lavender and put it up there. There are several years of lavender up above the door. It was because of looking out at the garden so often, through the door over there, that I made *Nathalie Granger*. For me, *Nathalie Granger* is that transparency, the transparency of the room in general.

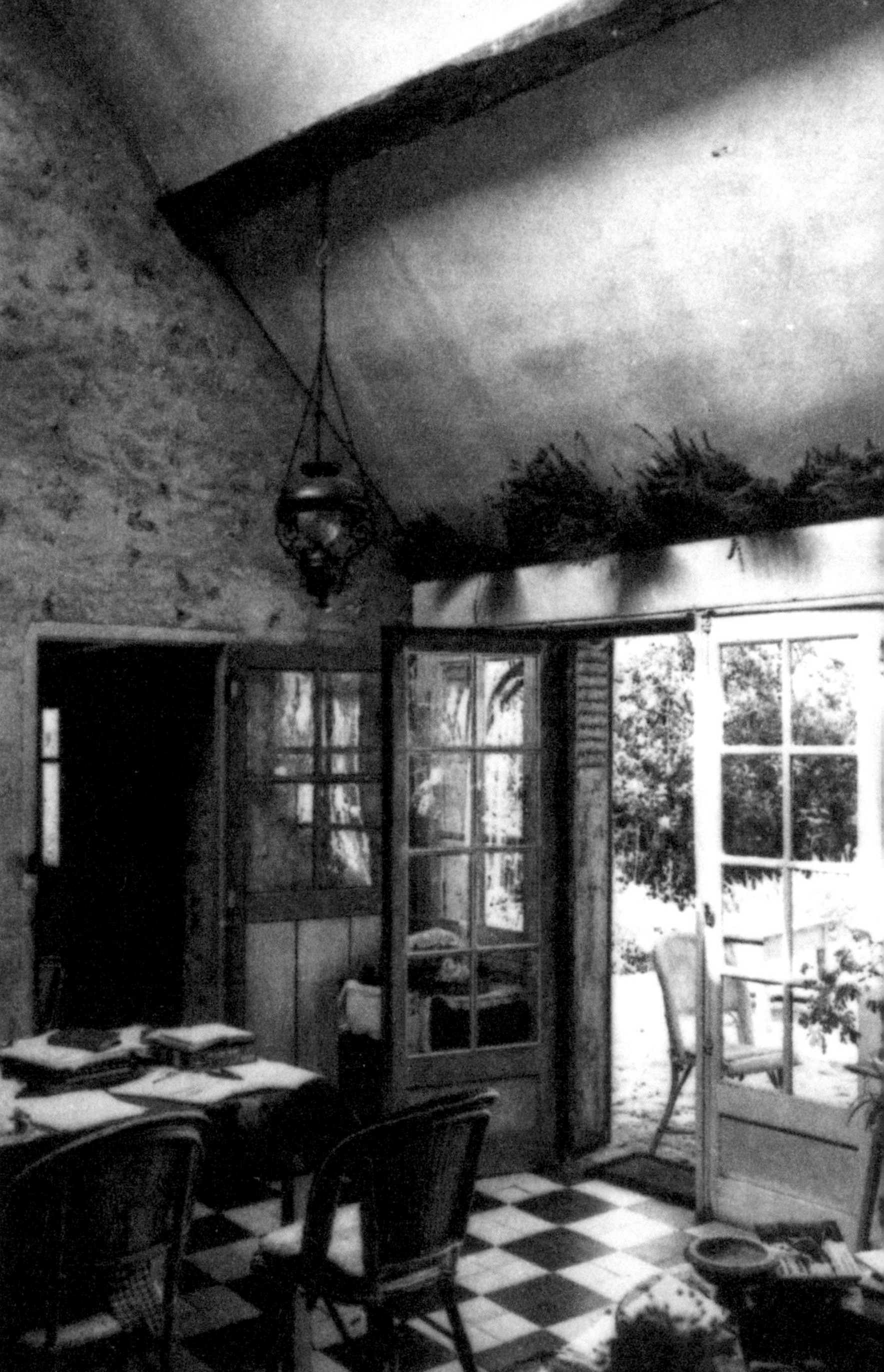

M. D. :
People always think that you need to start with a story to make a film, but that's not true. With *Nathalie Granger*, my starting point was the house. Completely. Truly, entirely. I had the house in my head, constantly, constantly, and then a story came to live there. But, you see, the house itself was already cinema.

A strange thing happened to me recently. I was alone in the house. I'd just done some laundry in the little kitchen at the end of the hall there, near the little girl's bedroom. It was very quiet, early autumn, going on for evening, and a big fly appeared. It swirled around inside the lampshade for a long time and at a certain point, it died. It fell, it was dead, and I remember noticing the time of its death, it must have been 5:55. Already, it was cinema, I was inside of a film. Maybe it was the story of the fly, or the story of me listening to the fly, I don't know, but I was in some other place entirely while still being there. It had already been transported somewhere else, you see? Sublimated, I think people, other people, say.

Yes, for *L'Après-midi de Monsieur Andesmas*, I'd seen a house above Saint-Tropez, near Gassin, that a friend of mine had bought. He showed me the place, on a hill facing the sea. It was a place that really took hold of me, and for six months I had it in my head, as if it were really, you know, lodged inside my head. It was empty for six months, empty, and, all of a sudden, someone came along, a very old man, and it was Mr. Andesmas. And I had the impression that if I waited here, if I locked myself in here, people would come along, and that would be another film. It's not reasonable, I can't make six or seven films like that in a row. That's what people told me. My friends said: There you go again, going on about that… that house. Not that house again! I don't know what other people use as their starting point. When they start with a story, I'm suspicious. I'm suspicious of a story that is already finished, even before the writing has begun—completely finished, with a beginning, middle, and end, with twists and turns. I don't trust it. I'm never quite sure where I'm headed. If I knew, I wouldn't write, because everything would be finished, already finished. I don't understand how anyone can write a story that's already been completely explored, itemized, mapped out. This seems to me so sad, and, I must say, destitute… but, well… it's probably an entirely different kind of writing. I am probably wrong about this, at some level.

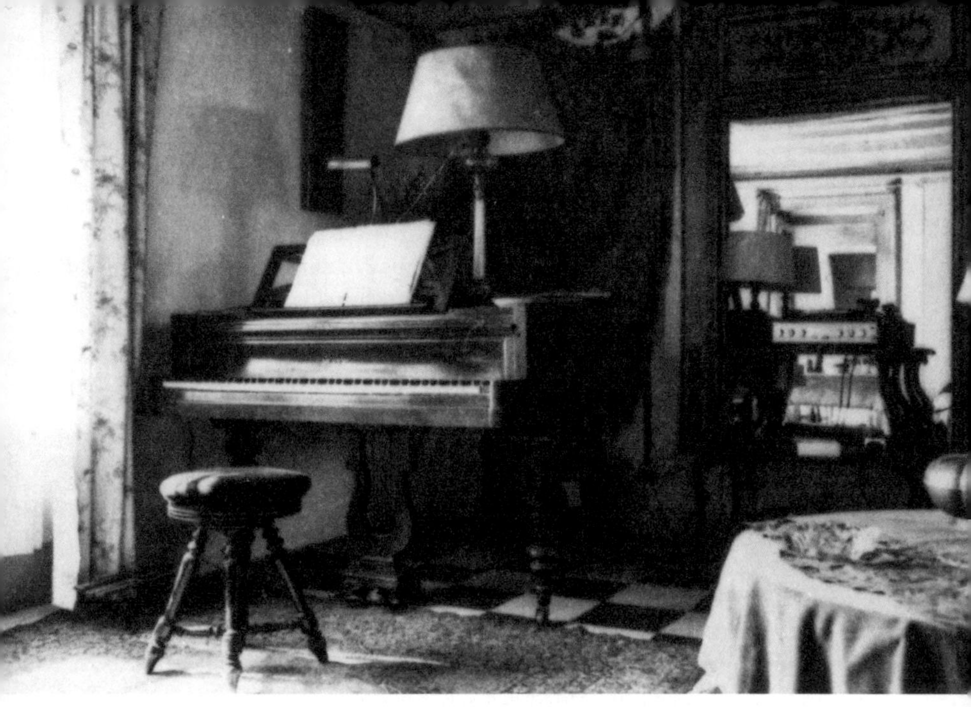

[*Marguerite Duras goes to sit down at the piano.*]

M. D. :
The actors in *Nathalie Granger* wanted to walk, or anyway to have a rhythm they could walk to, constantly, in the
house, and maintain the same pace. And in the end, their
steps were set to a few arpeggios that I'd played on the piano, which were gradually transformed and became the music for the film. I received royalties for that music. *(Laughs.)*

[*She plays a few notes from* Nathalie Granger.]
That's what it was originally.
[*She plays a piano exercise for children.*]
When I hear this, I can see Jeanne walking down the corridors. Jeanne Moreau. It's a very old piano. It can't even be tuned any longer, it's so worn out, but we love it. I don't play, or only very little, but my son plays a bit, his father plays a lot, and friends come over to play. And in the end, we have a very good time with the piano, we play duets until three in the morning. I really like this room, because it's completely transparent, and it's at the very end of the house, it's the last room. Very isolated.

I can reproduce the melody from *India Song* for you.
[*She plays the melody from* India Song.]
It's so that I don't lose contact with the piano, too. It means that I can still touch it, even with just one hand.

Though it's true that I always find it painful to hear someone play well. When people play very well, I'm enchanted, dazzled and despairing all at once.

We played up until here in *Nathalie…*
[*She plays* Nathalie Granger.]
Over the shot of the bedroom with the children's toys, you can hear the sound of the piano keys, the wood.
[*She plays the beginning of a Bach fugue with one hand.*]
People will think I play, but I don't… Can you still hear it?
[*She listens to the resonance for a long time.*
We hear the continuation of the fugue, on the closing credits,
FIN.]

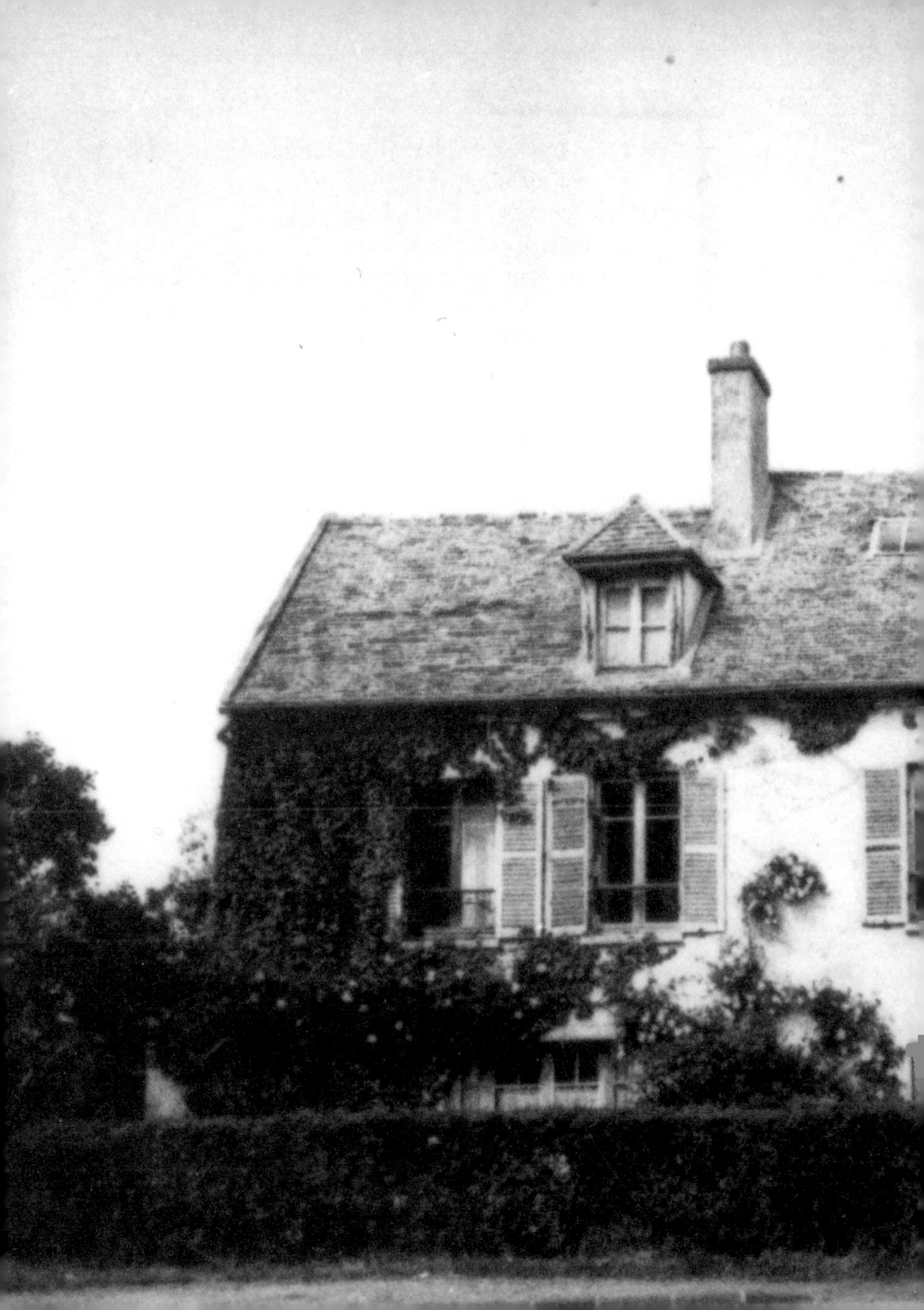

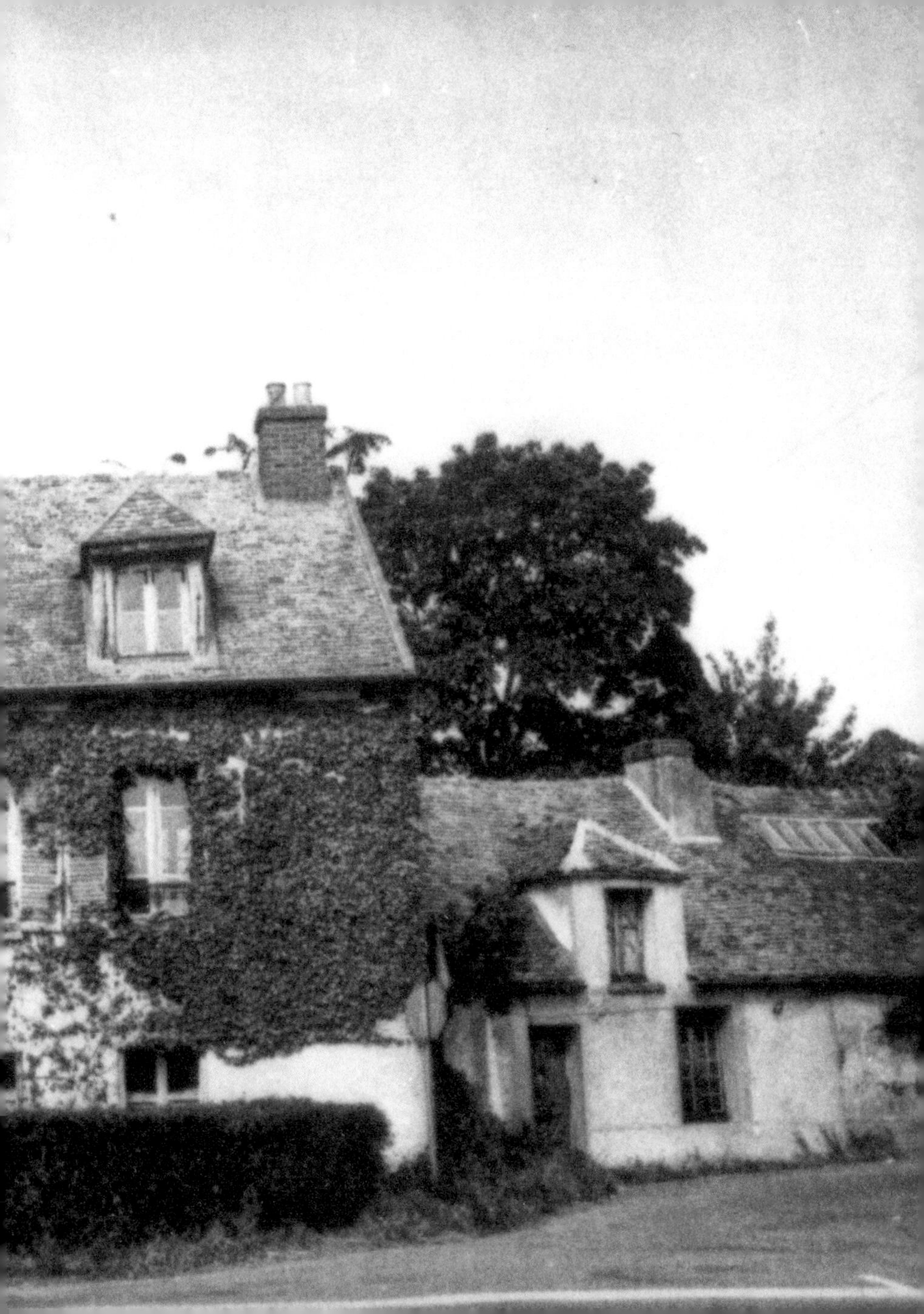

2

M. D. :
I'm eighteen in this one.

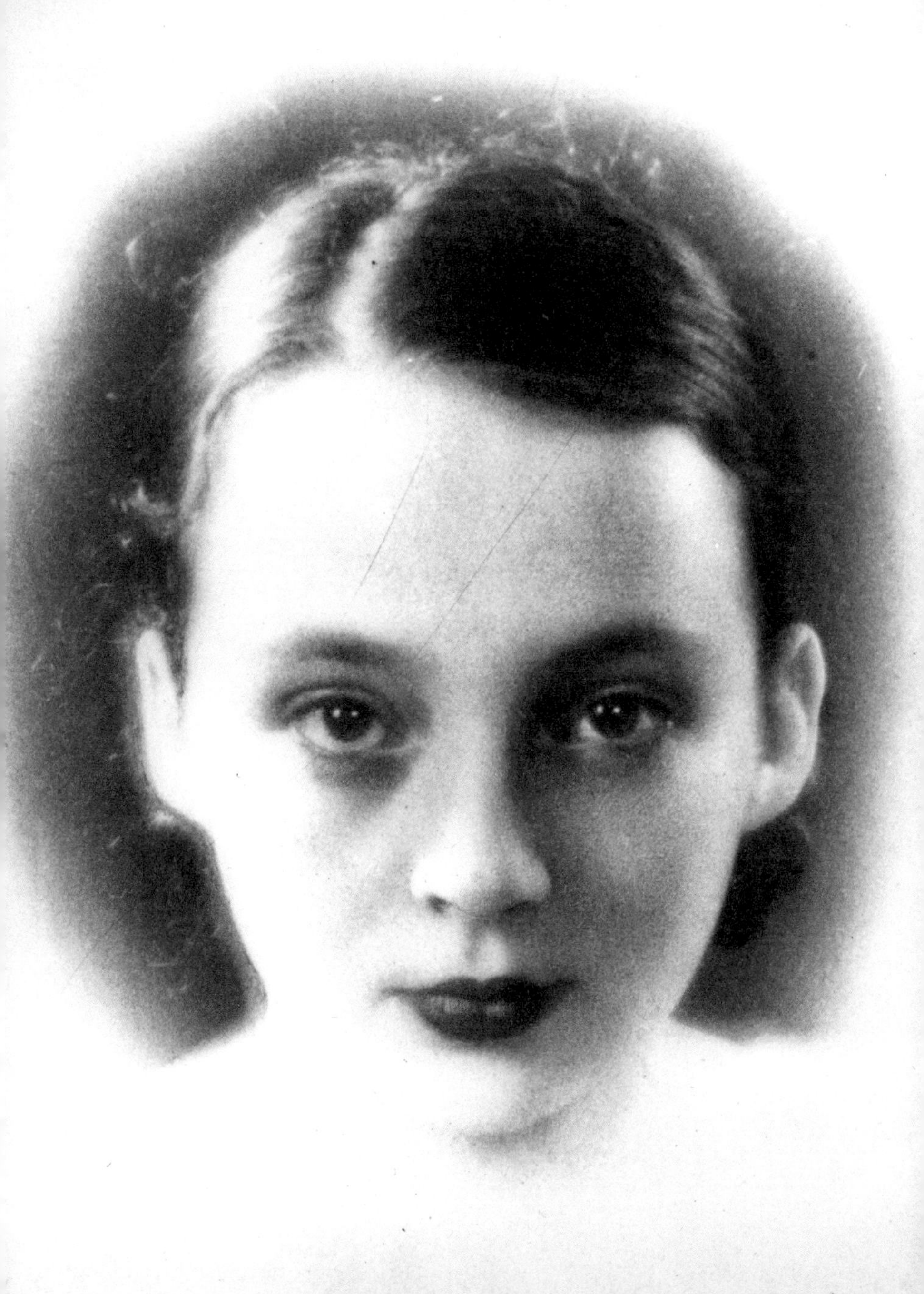

— Here, I'm sixteen. It's in Sa Đéc, by the Mekong. The dress
was green.

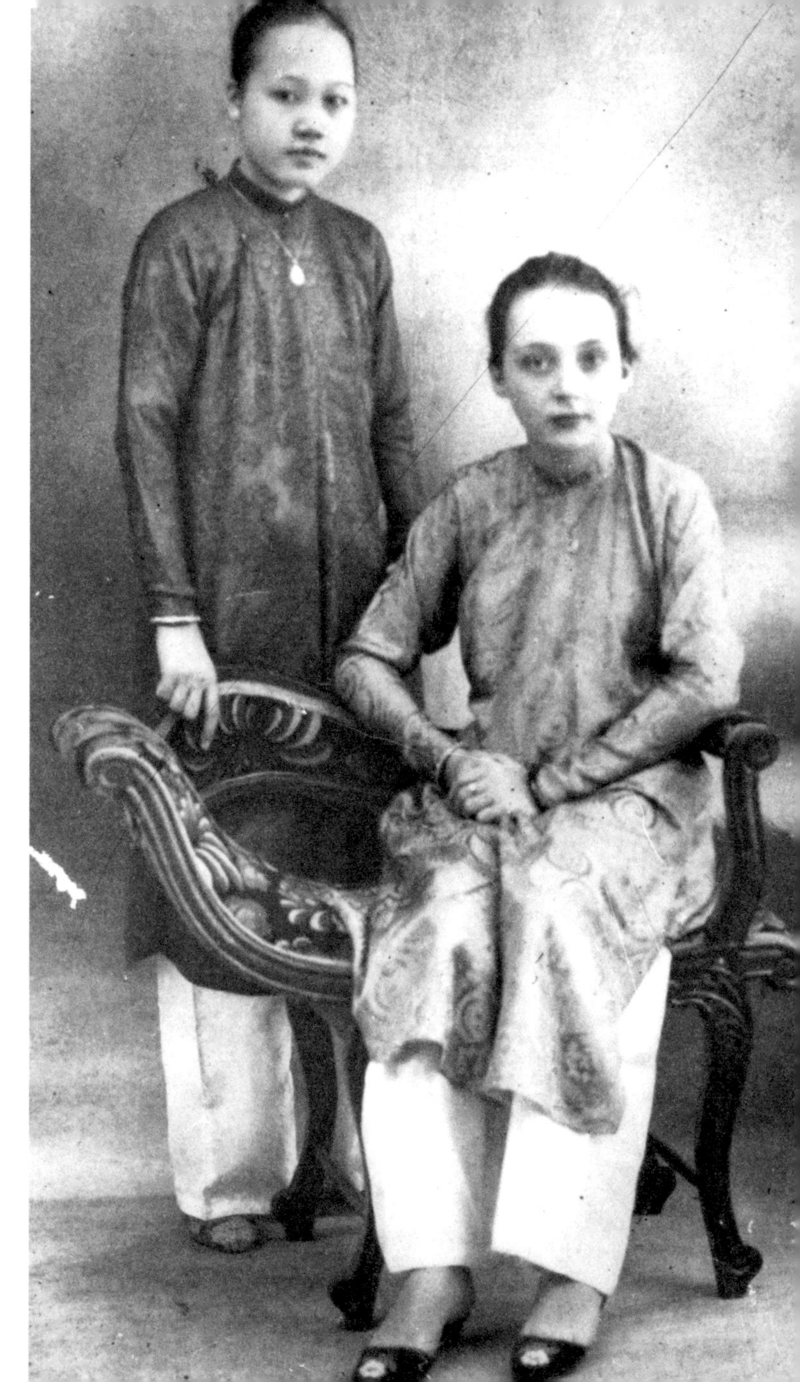

— Beside me is my brother, I called him Joseph in *Barrage sur le Pacifique*. He died very young during the war, due to a lack of medical supplies.

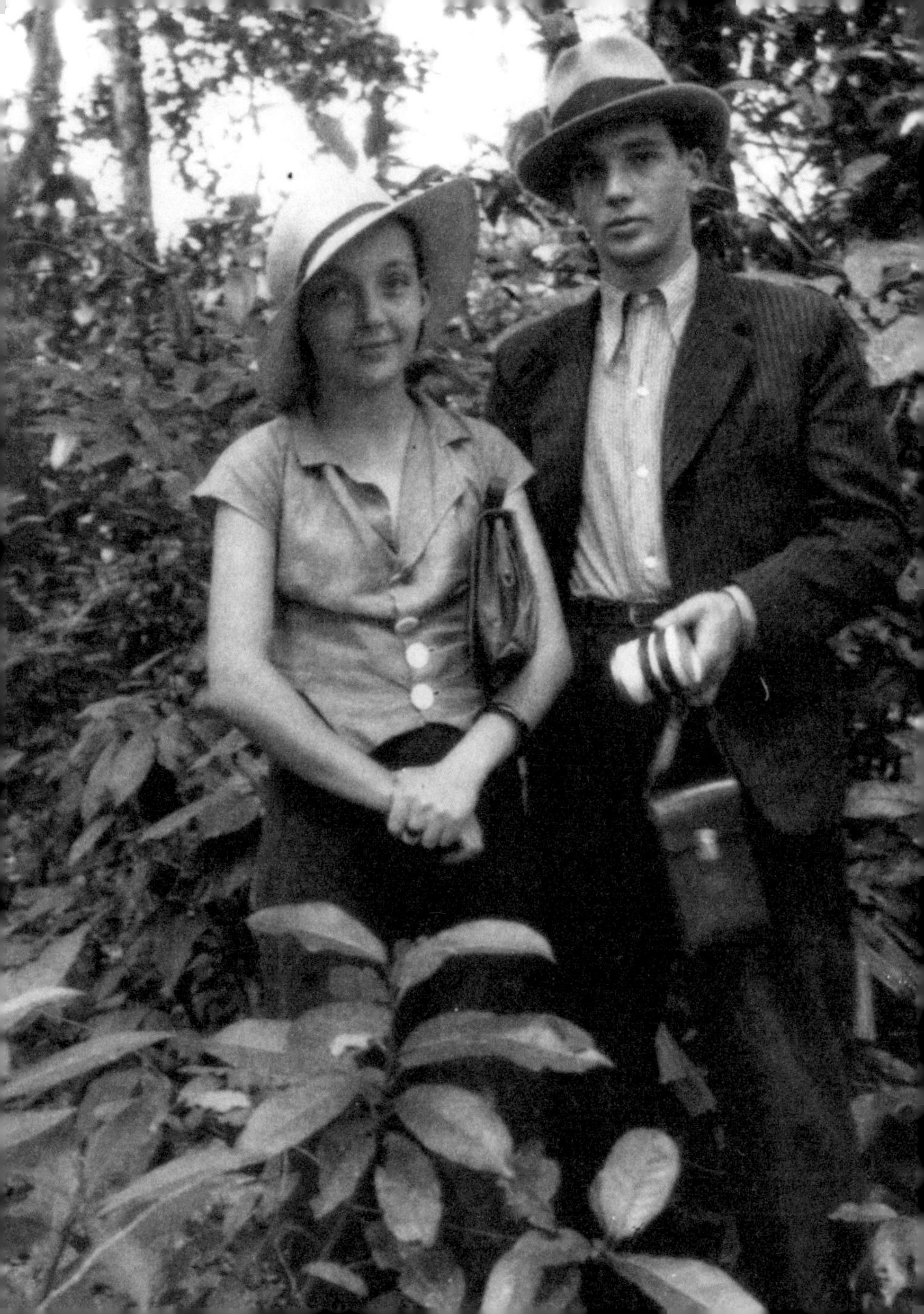

— I never knew my father. He died when I was four. He wrote a book of mathematics on exponential functions, which I lost. All I have left of him is this photograph and a postcard he wrote to his children before he died.

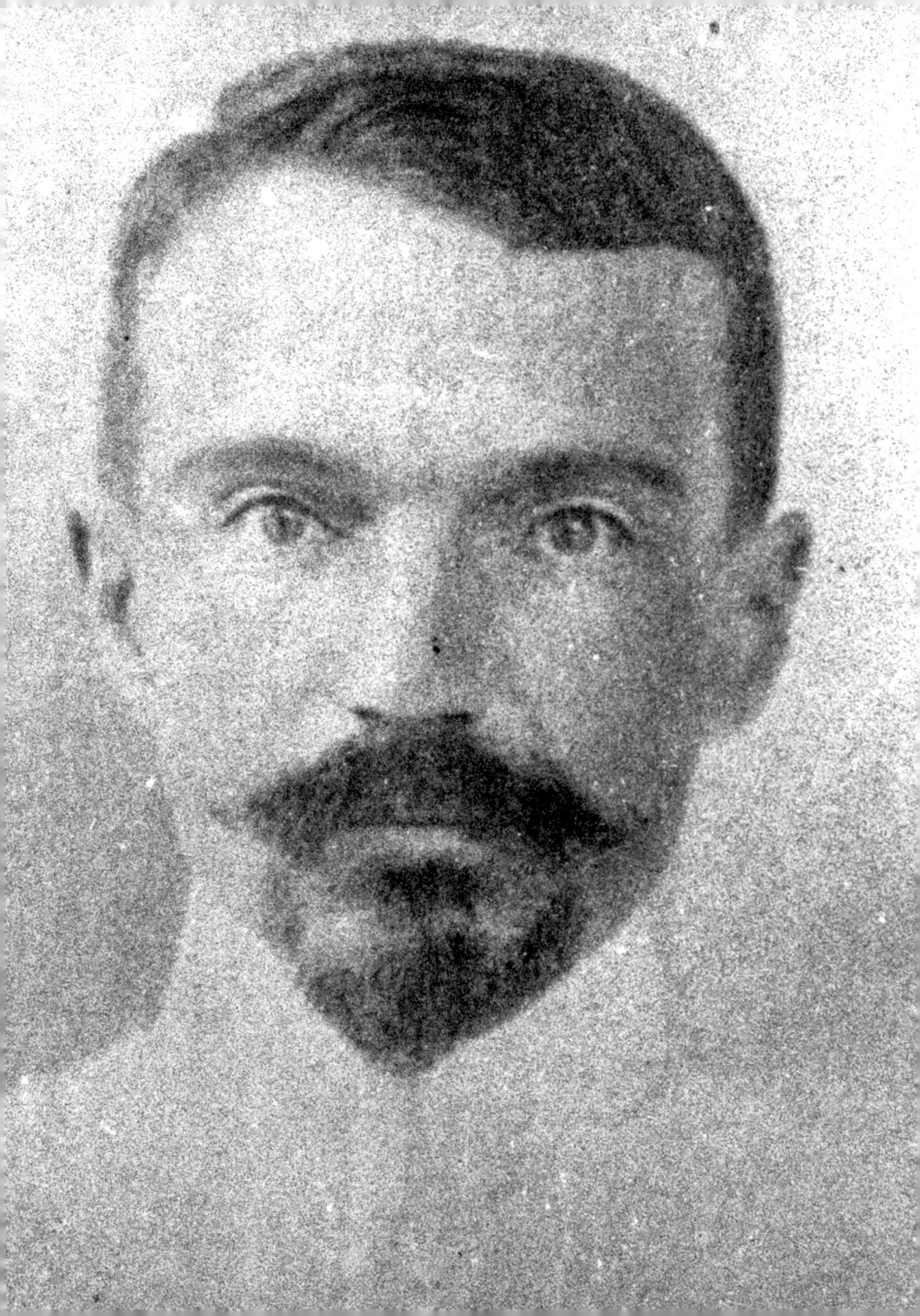

— My mother.

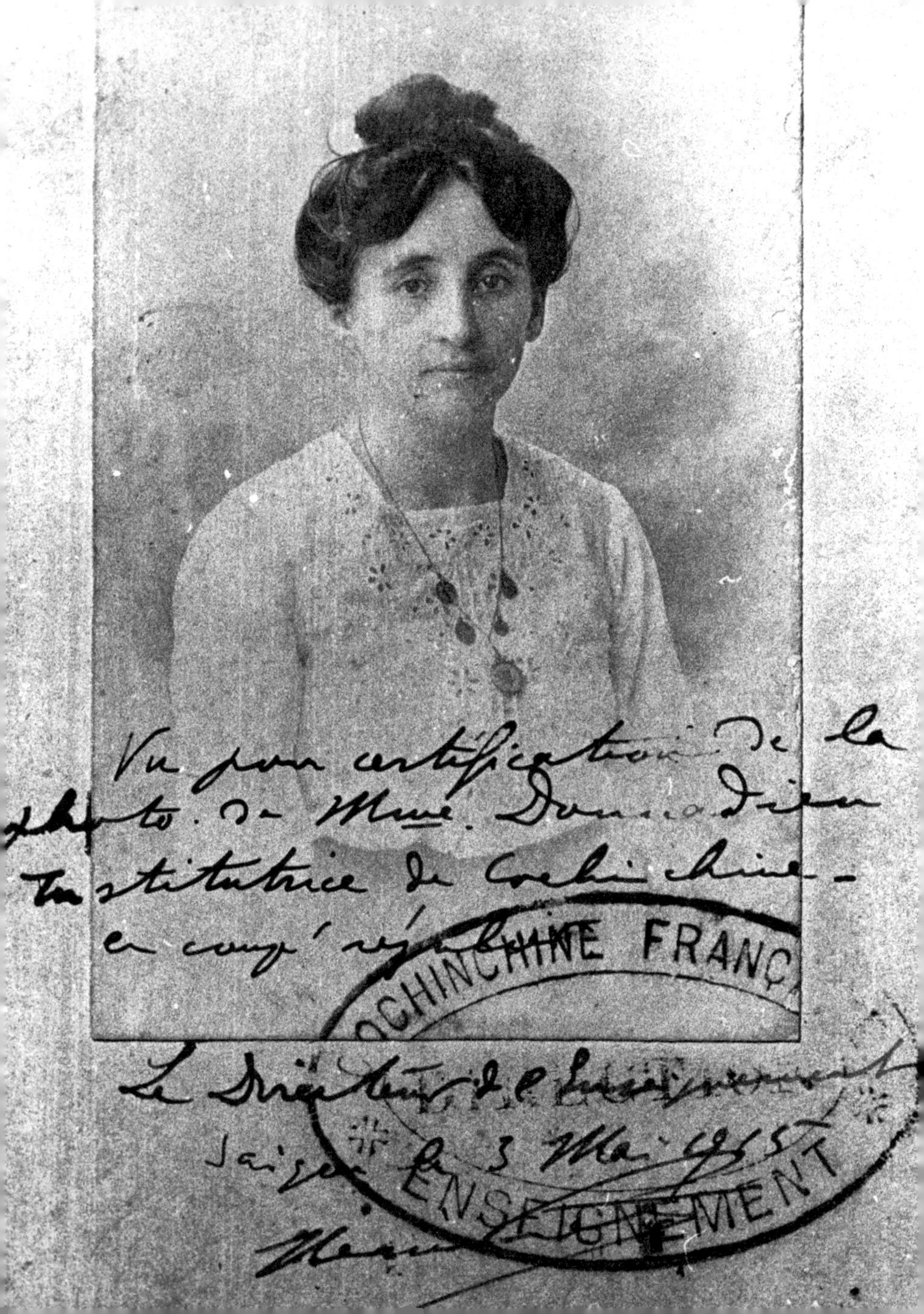

Vu pour certification de la
photo. de Mme Donnadieu
institutrice de Cochinchine –
en congé régulier

Le Directeur de l'Enseignement
Saigon le 3 Mai 1925

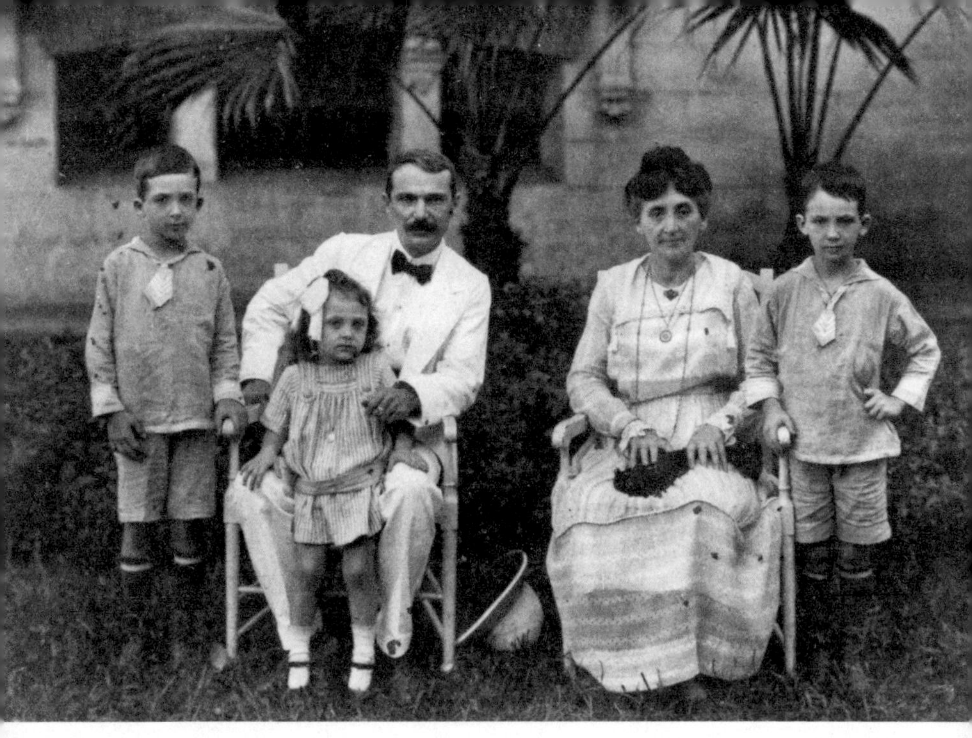

— I had two brothers.

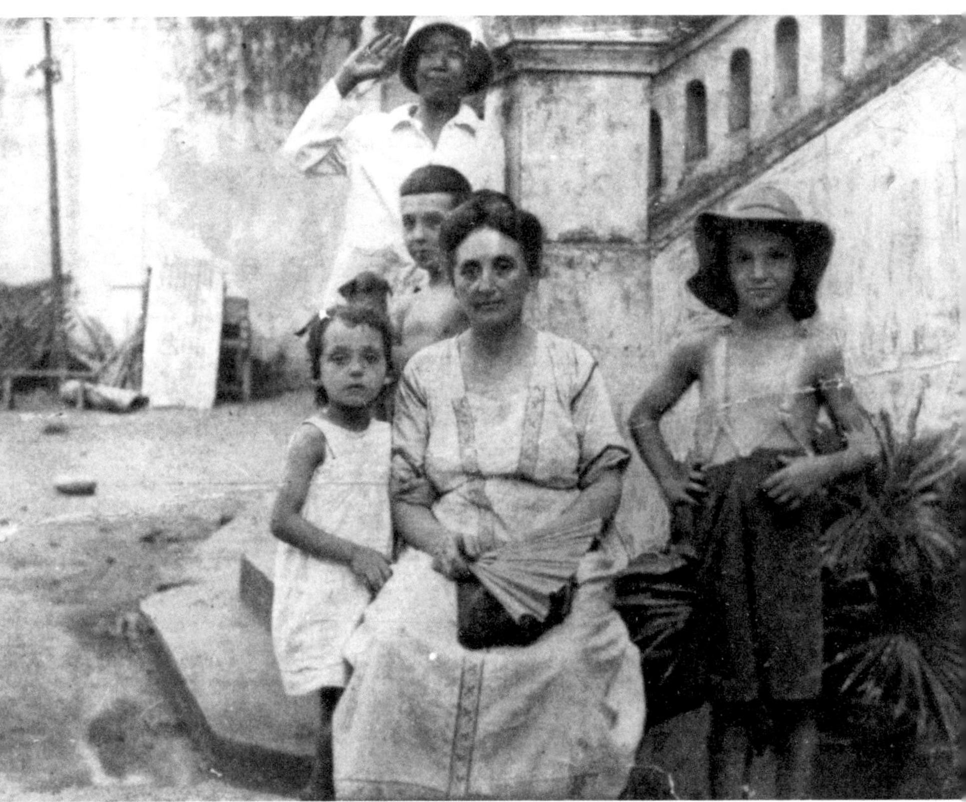

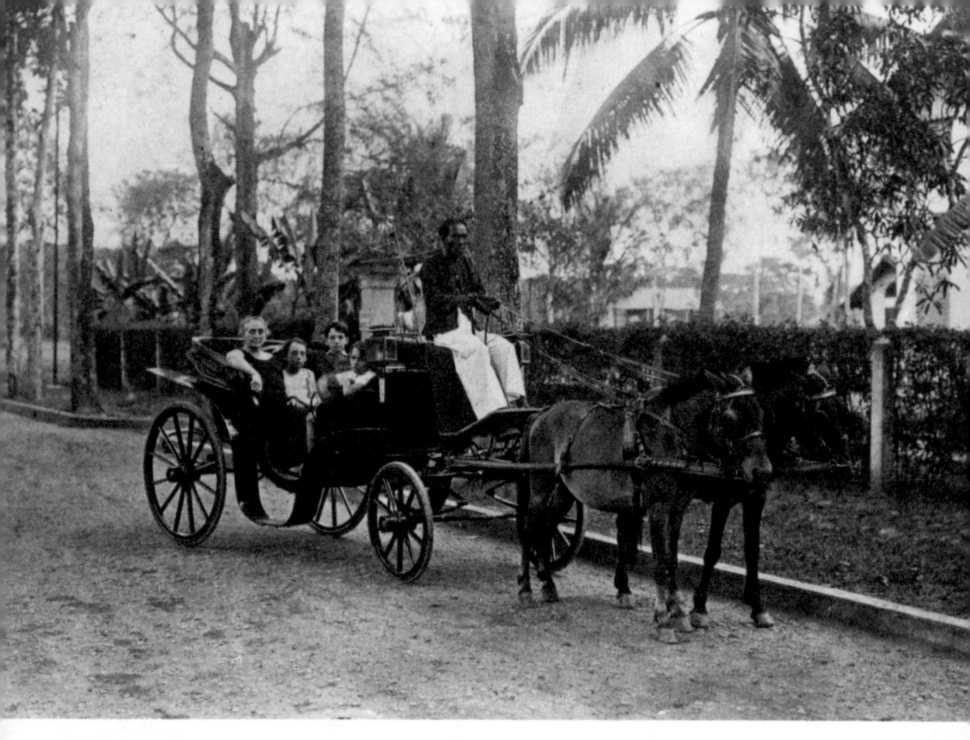

— This is a horse-drawn carriage we used to go out in at night, in Vĩnh Long. I remember that we passed a lazaretto and crossed some rice fields and then came back along the banks of the Mekong. Night would be falling as we made our way home.

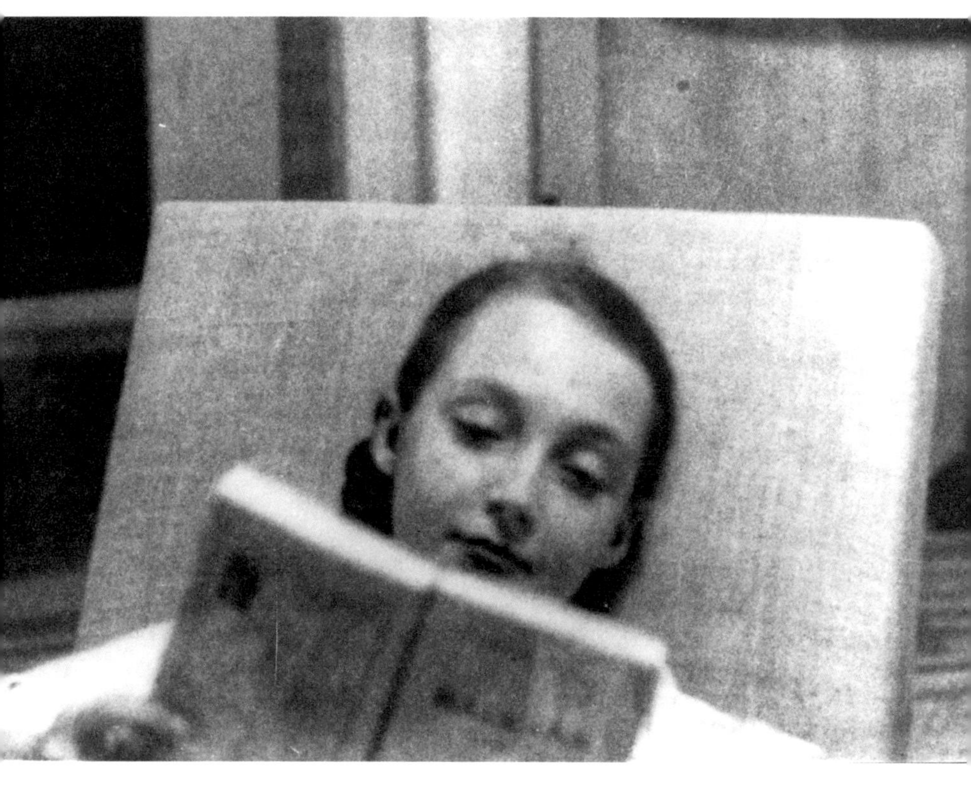

M. P. :

Marguerite, one day you told me that your mother was closer
to any Vietnamese peasant woman than to the women of white
society

M. D. :

Yes. She was a peasant, she was from a peasant background, she
had been a peasant. She attended teacher's college as a schol-
arship student, but her parents were farmers in the north. And
then, because we were very, very poor and her job was one of the
lowest you could have over there (along with customs officers and
postal workers, the teachers in the indigenous schools were at the
bottom of the ladder in white society), she was much closer to the
Vietnamese, the Annamese, than to other white people. All my
friends were Vietnamese until I was fourteen or fifteen, yes.

After twenty years of working in the civil service, she bought a
plot of land in Cambodia around Kampot.

M. P. :

A concession?

M. D. :

What people called a concession, yes. And she was given,
they saw this woman arriving alone, a widow… with no one to
defend her, completely isolated, and they stuck her with a piece
of non-arable land. She had absolutely no idea that you had to
bribe the land registry agents to get workable land. She was given
a plot of land, but it wasn't land, it was a piece of ground that was
under water for six months of the year. And she put twenty years of
savings into it. So she had this bungalow built, she sowed seeds, she
transplanted rice, and after three months, the Pacific rose and we
were ruined. She nearly died, she went off the rails, she had seizures,

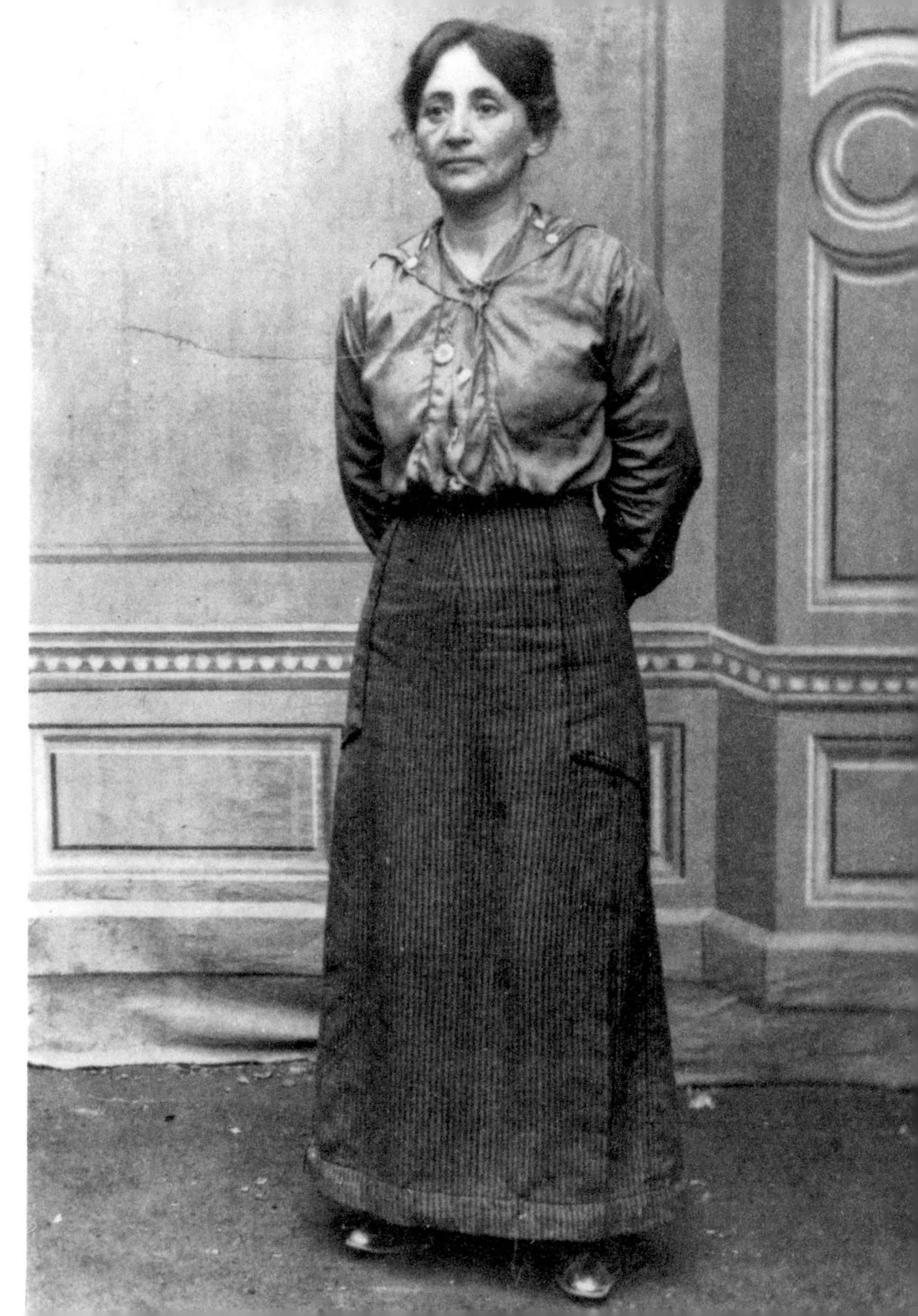

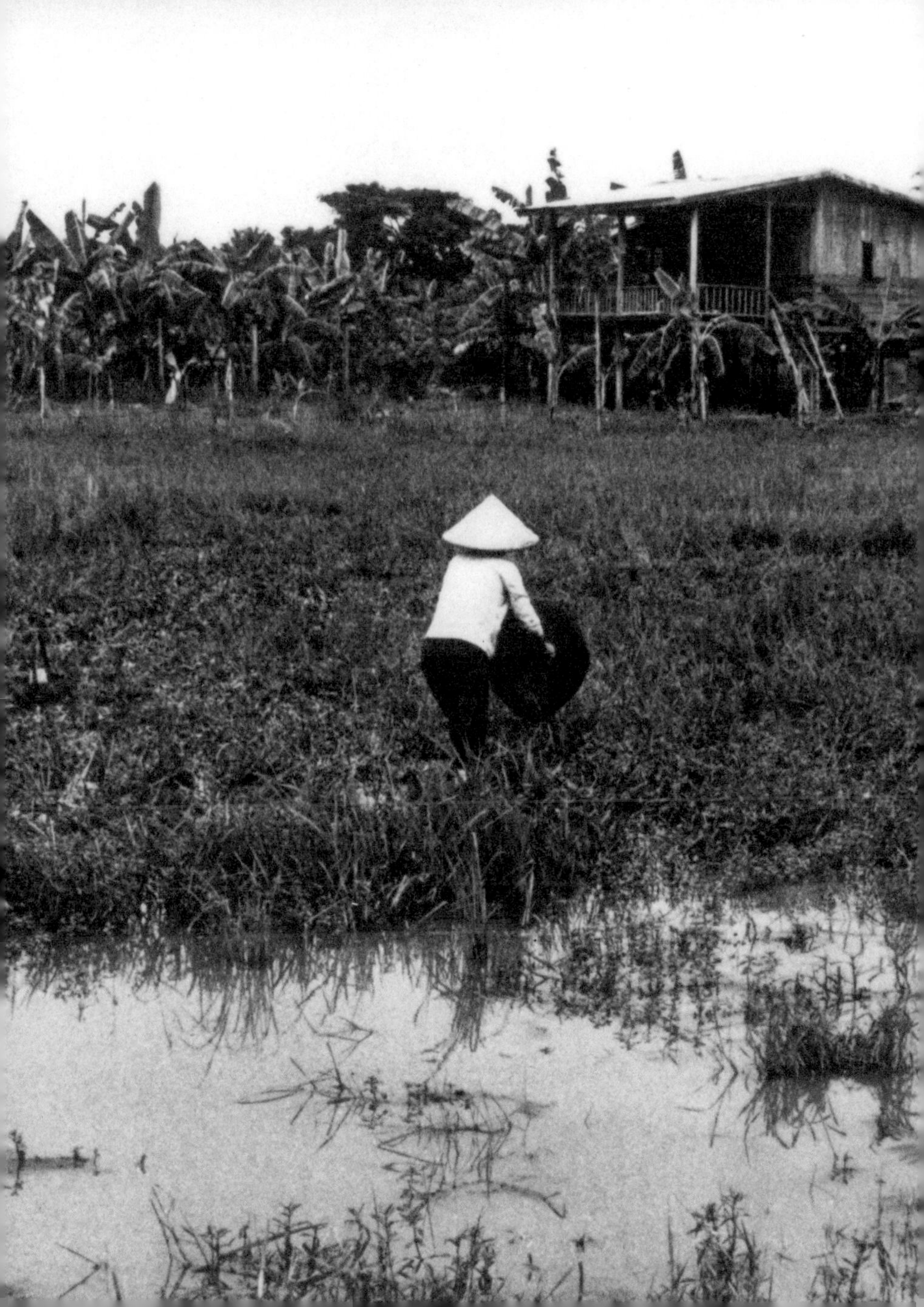

fits like those of epilepsy. She lost her mind. We thought she was going to die. I think that after the sea walls collapsed, she almost died or was dying from anger, to tell the truth. From anger. From indignation. Of course, the effect on us was dreadful. I can't talk about it calmly even now, you see. She lodged a complaint, she was up in arms, but corruption at the time was terrible. And we realized that everyone at the land registry, from the agents to the general administrator of the colony, were all lining their pockets. In other words, bribes were spread throughout the civil service hierarchy. Complaints went by the boards—they ended up in drawers—and she died without having won. Yes, injustice was complete.

There was a sort of plain, but quite high up, a kind of plateau, and to the north there were the Elephant Mountains, and to the south was a land where there were no more villages, no dwellings, a land of water, of marshes. Mangrove forests by the sea were all that could be seen above the water for hundreds of hectares during the rainy season. But still, it was childhood, or anyway, my childhood, the years I spent there with the younger of my brothers, the one I called Joseph in the book. I had two brothers. The older one and I were not together much as children. Because my mother couldn't raise all three of us after my father's death, my eldest brother stayed in France to attend a school for electricians, as I recall. She kept the two younger children with her. You understand, she was so overcome with despair, and what she was living through was so abominable, that her despair consumed all of her attention, and our freedom was absolute. I've never seen children as free as my brother and me, on the land around the sea wall. She didn't have time to take care of us. I don't believe she thought about her children anymore, so we'd run off and stay away for days on end. Not in the trees *(laughs)* but in the forest, on the rivers—on the racs, what we called the racs, those little streams that flow down to the sea. We hunted. It made for a childhood very different from the kind you have here. We were more Vietnamese than French, you see. What I'm starting to realize is that our kinship with the French race—excuse me, with French nationality—was false. We spoke Vietnamese like little Vietnamese children, never wore shoes, we went around half-naked, we bathed in the river. My mother, of course, never spoke Vietnamese, she never managed to learn. It's very difficult. I passed my baccalaureate in Vietnamese. One day, I *learned* that I was French, you see… Mother often said to us, "You, who are French" and so on. One day, she went to Saigon and brought back some reinette apples. Or what are they called, those red apples called?

M. P. :

I don't know.

M. D. :

And she forced us to eat them. We couldn't swallow them, we said it was like eating cotton wool, that they weren't edible, that we couldn't eat French food. I had a kind of anorexia when I was ten, in Phnom Penh. I was forced to eat steak and I vomited it up. We came from over there, the back of beyond, really. Oh, it must happen often, you're in a certain environment, in a given space; you're born in that environment, you speak the language of the environment, and so on—the first games I ever played were Vietnamese games, with Vietnamese children—and then you are told that you're not Vietnamese, and have to stop seeing Vietnamese children because they're not French, and you have to wear shoes, eat steak frites and behave in such and such a way. I realized this very late, maybe just now, you see. I also lived for years in Sa Đéc and Vĩnh Long.

M. P. :

Near the Mekong?

M. D. :

Yes, on the Mekong. These are posts where white people lived, with perpendicular streets, gardens, fences, and then there's the river, the French Circle, the tennis courts, and Anne-Marie Stretter, yes, probably, in Vĩnh Long, the wife of the ambassador.

One day, a government launch stops.
Monsieur Stretter is inspecting the Mekong posts.

Takes her away to Savannakhet?

Yes. Takes her with him.
For seventeen years, through the capitals of Asia.

You find her in Peking.
Again in Mandalay...
You find her in Bangkok.
In Rangoon.
In Sydney.
You find her in Lahore.
Seventeen years.
She's in Calcutta...
Calcutta...
She dies.

(India Song)

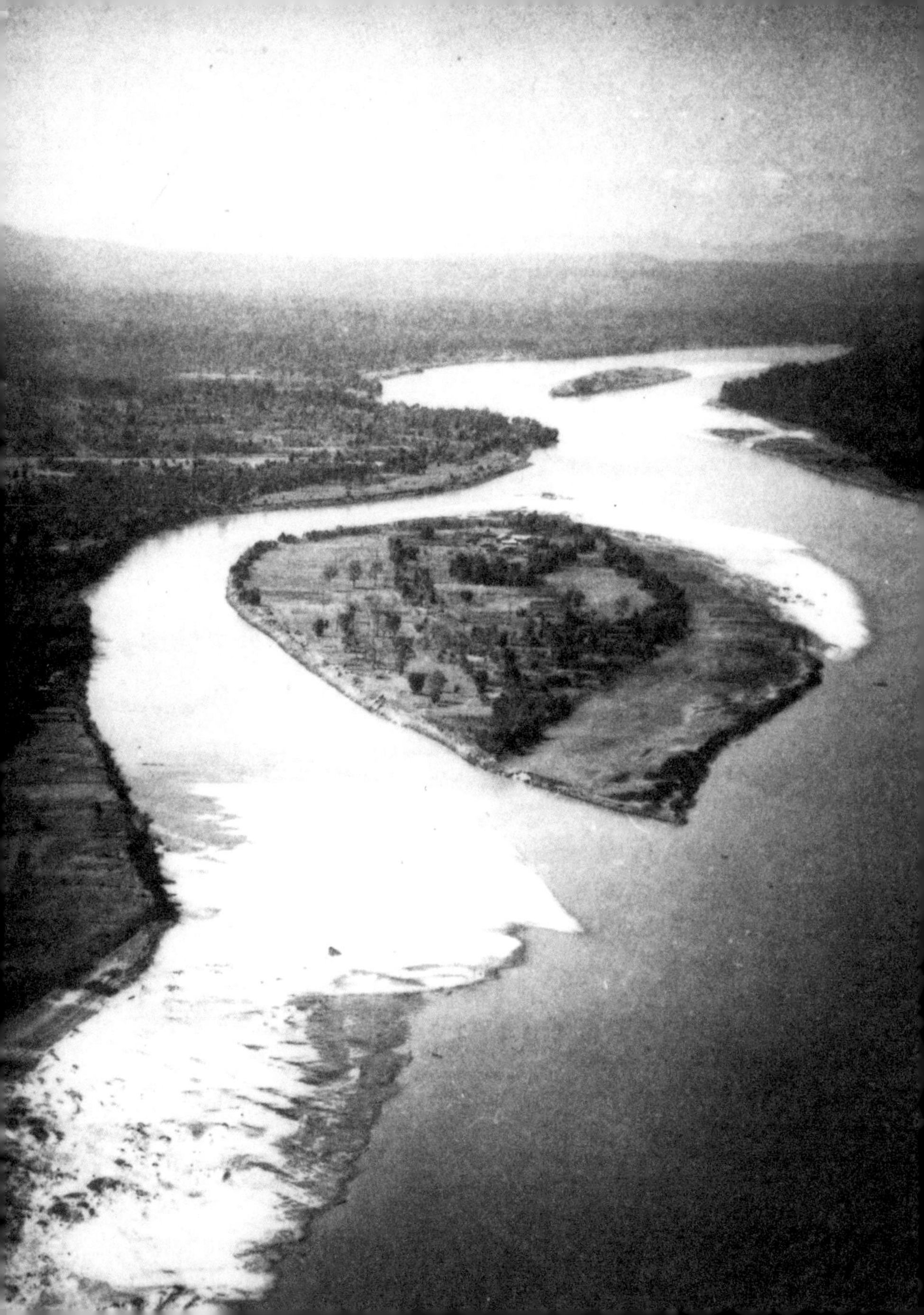

M. D.:

For all I know, that was her real name. I don't think I invented it. Or maybe I distorted it, you see, or it really was her name, Stretter. She was a redhead, I remember. She didn't wear make-up, she was very pale, very white, and had two little girls.

M. P.:

Did you know her?

M. D.:

I never spoke to her.


```
How white she is!
How white they are, the women of Calcutta!
For six months they only go out in the evening,
fleeing the sun.
She seems imprisoned in a kind of suffering.
No one really knows what goes on behind these walls...
  what she does.
```

(India Song)

M. D.:

It was a long time ago, I don't know exactly. I used to see her drive by in the evening in her car with her chauffeur. When it was cooler, she'd go out.

Shortly after she arrived, we learned that a young man had committed suicide for love of her. I remember the upheaval this provoked in me. Nothing made sense anymore. The shock I felt, which was very intense, on hearing the story, came from the fact that apparently, this woman was not a fashionable or sociable woman. She had an invisible quality, the opposite of showy, very quiet, not known to have friends, and she always walked alone or with her two little girls, as in the book *The Vice-Consul*. Then, out of the blue, we heard that story. If you like, for a long time, for me, she embodied a kind of twofold power: a power of death and an everyday power. She raised children, she was the ambassador's wife, she played tennis, entertained, walked, etc. But there was also this power of death in her, death-giving power, the power to provoke death. Sometimes I think I began writing because of her.

M. P. :

In *India Song*, is it your fascination whose spell we are under?

M. D. :

What is being staged is my fascination with her, my love of her. I ask myself if my love has not always existed, and if my idea of a parent was not based on her, on Anne-Marie Stretter, the mother of two little girls, instead of my own mother, who seemed to me too mad and too exuberant—which, by the way, she was. It was that secret power. You had to possess secret power to have that kind of strength in life. I think that's what she was, Anne-Marie Stretter, my idea of a parent, of a mother—of a woman, rather. She didn't strike me as maternal. First and foremost, she was an adulteress, you see, not the mother of little girls.

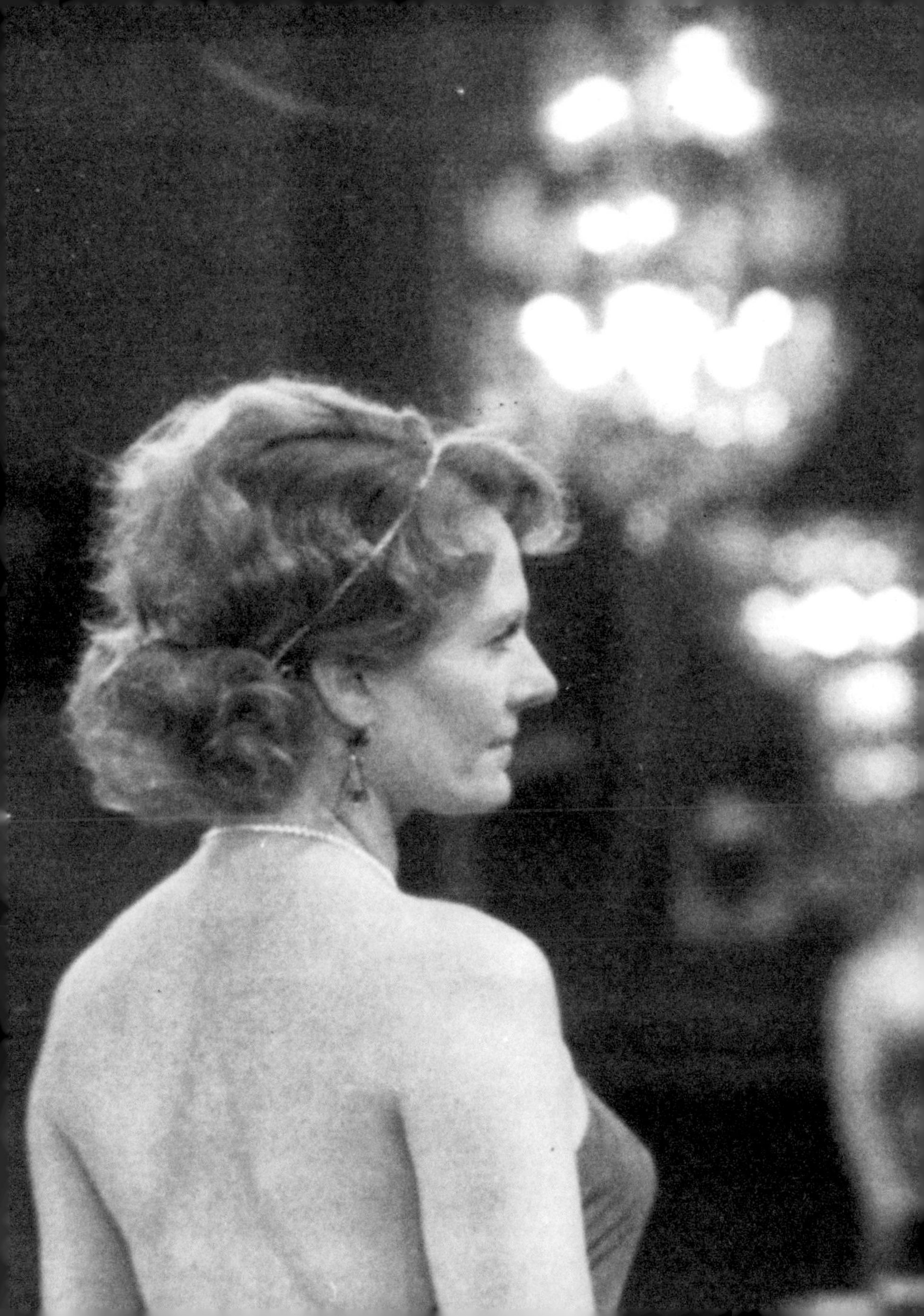

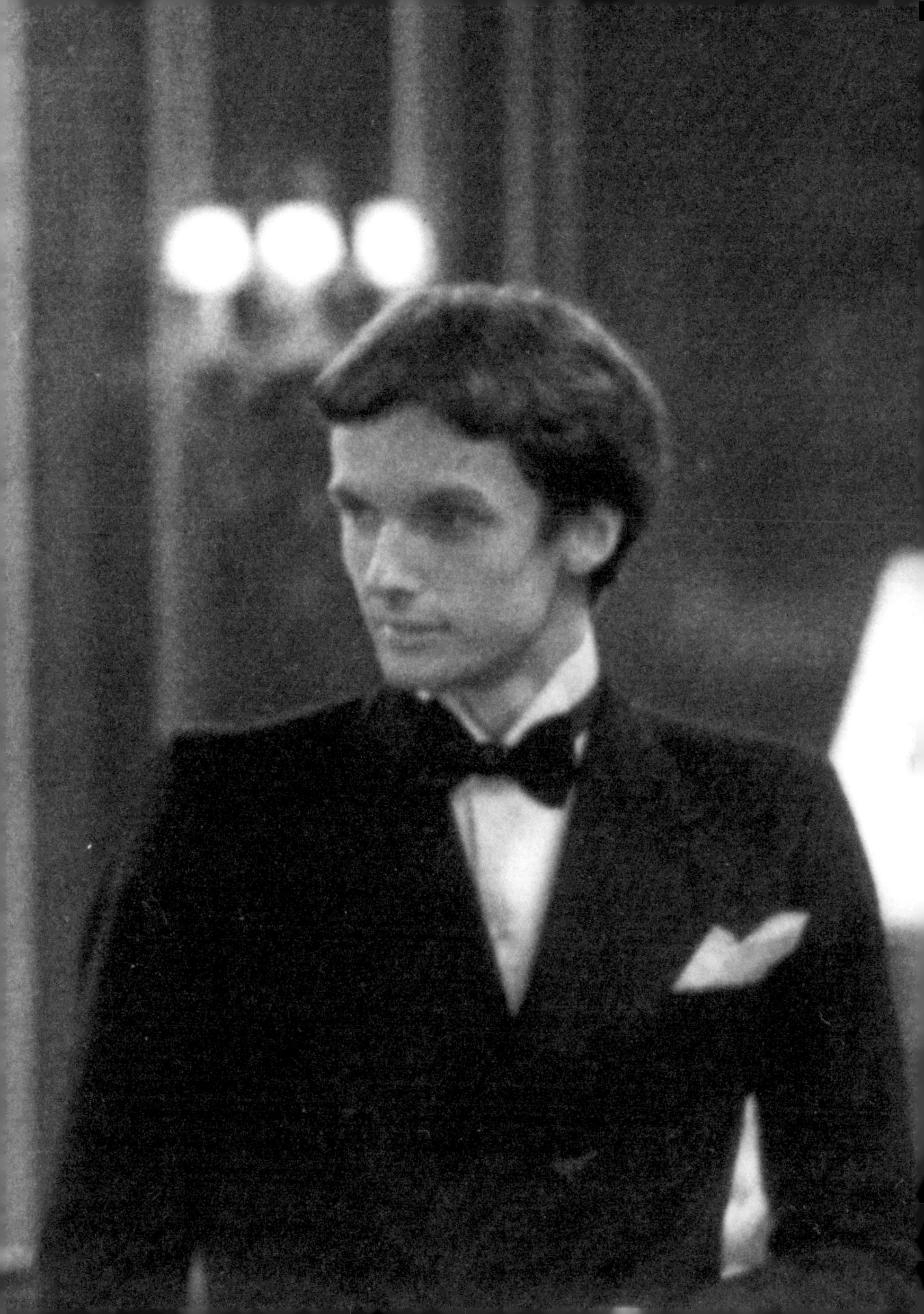

Anne-Marie Stretter:
You know, one could say almost nothing is... is possible
in India...
The young attaché:
What do you mean?
Anne-Marie Stretter:
Oh... nothing... this general despondency...
It's neither painful nor pleasant to live in India.
Neither easy nor difficult. It's nothing... you see?
Nothing.
The young attaché:
You mean it's impossible?
Anne-Marie Stretter:
Well... perhaps, yes...
But then, you know it's probably an over-simplification.

(India Song)

M. D. :

She's talking about India, yes. Maybe that's where it all comes from. She no longer says anything, by which I mean that she is no longer preoccupied by anything to do with herself. She has no more personal preoccupations or problems to speak of. I think that's what it is. Anne-Marie Stretter is a thousand years old, she has lived a thousand years. Which is where the sovereignty of women comes from. Men are rarely able to attain it. Because her silence is twofold: there's the silence of women in general and there's the silence that comes from her life, her person. This doubleness, the conjugation of these two silences may be, or even quite certainly is, Anne-Marie Stretter. I ask myself whether the other women in my books did not conceal her for a long time, and if Anne-Marie Stretter had not been there all along behind Lol V. Stein. Because there's no rhyme nor reason to this fascination, I can't get free of it. It's a true love story.

For years, my films and books have been love affairs with her. But not all the time. There are times when I don't think about her; when I'm making other films, I don't think about her. But she's still there.

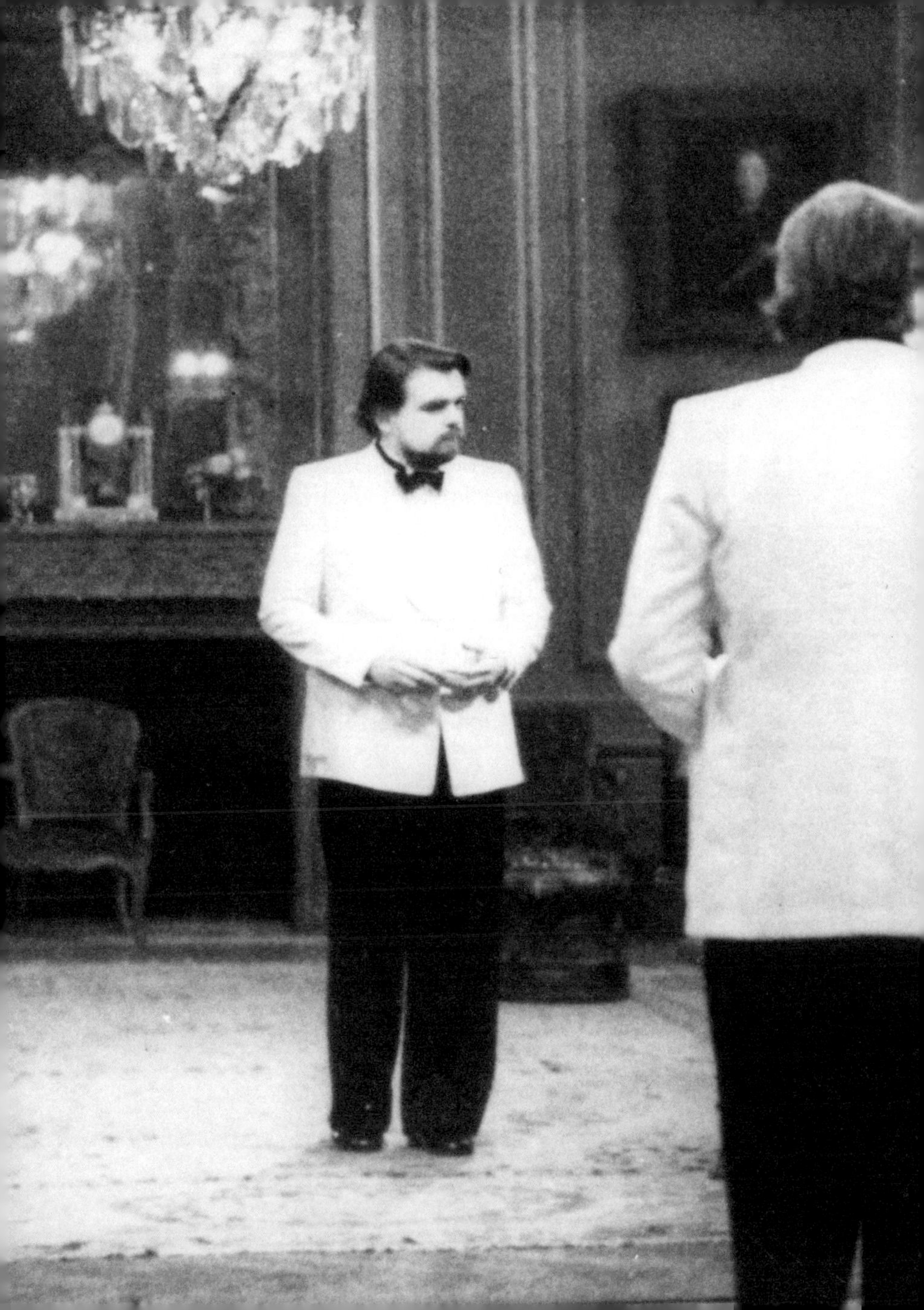

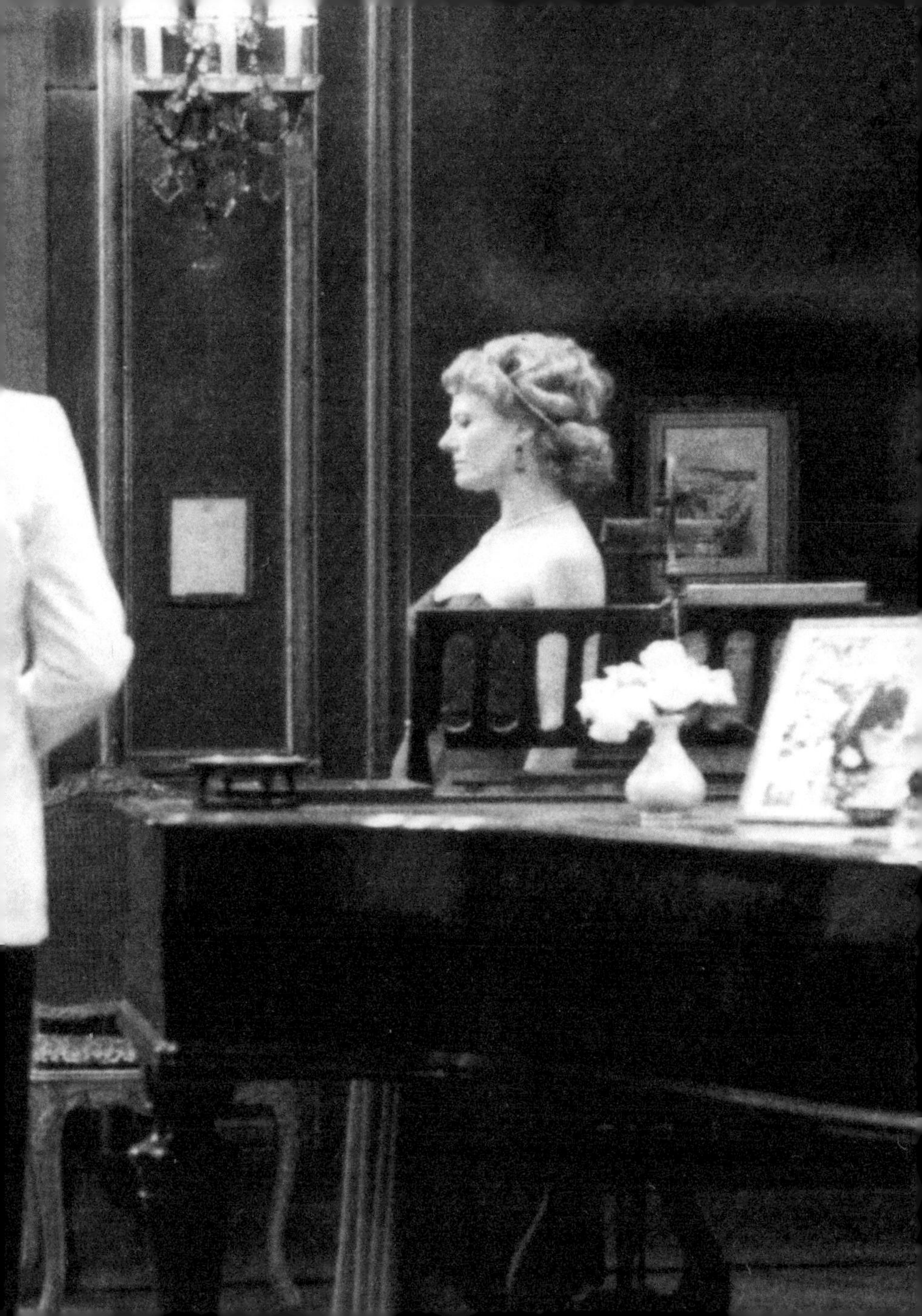

M. D. :

In the middle of the image, right in the middle is what I call the altar to the memory of Anne-Marie Stretter. It serves a dual purpose. It is my place, by which I mean it's the place of my pain, the pain of my inability to bring her back from death, from a death I've caused, and it's the place of my love for her. This altar receives external—objective—upkeep. A servant comes to relight the incense and bring fresh roses. It's an altar, and Delphine Seyrig goes to it and looks at the photograph of a dead woman, and even in the script, at one point, it says that she goes towards the photograph as if she were being looked at by the photo. I see a gaze that is twofold. We never get very close to the photo of the dead woman. It remains barely legible.

M. P. :
Do mirrors play a major role in all your films?
M. D. :
Yes, they're like holes in which the image is devoured and from which it reemerges. I never know where it will resurface. I have the impression that Delphine is swallowed whole and then reappears; she reappears or she doesn't, but what intense pleasure it gives to see Delphine reappear so far away. With a mirror, the image can be infinitely distanced. It's as if she were arriving from the end of cinema—I was going to say from the ends of the earth, but it's from the end of cinema, when she reappears in the mirror.

M. P. :

Is the mirror there to safeguard distance, a distance that no longer exists?

M. D. :

Yes, or rather to cast doubt.

M. P. :

On real presence?

M. D. :

Yes, on real presence and speech. When the vice-consul says, "Calcutta has become a form of hope for me," I don't know whether he is speaking to Anne-Marie Stretter as a person, or as an emblem, or to the emblematic reach of Anne-Marie Stretter. I think that's what it is. There's an extension of the field, you see, the field of speech. Which means that words are no longer solely addressed to the subject who is present.

M. D. :

I think that Anne-Marie Stretter has surpassed all analysis, you see, all questioning. She has surpassed all the prejudice about intelligence and knowledge, about theory. She's a kind of despair, universal despair that coincides with deep political despair and is lived as such, calmly. I once said that she was Calcutta, I see her as Calcutta. She becomes Calcutta, there's a double shift: Calcutta moves towards the form of Anne-Marie Stretter, and Anne-Marie Stretter moves towards the form of Calcutta. And at the end of the film, I see them as forming a single entity.

I'm not saying she's a liberated woman. I'm saying that she's on a very sure path to liberation, a very personal, individual path to liberation. It is through embracing the world in the most general sense—the world in its generality, if you will—that she is the most herself. It is through being fully open to everything in Calcutta, to poverty, hunger, love, prostitution, and desire, that she is the most herself. That's who Anne-Marie Stretter is. When I say "prostitution," I mean that prostitution passes through her, like hunger, tears, and desire. She is a hollow form, a receptacle; things come to inhabit her and then move on. That's what I mean when I talk about Anne-Marie Stretter's liberation. But you know, it's quite possible that I'm on shaky ground here and I will never know why she has such a hold on me. It is like being engulfed by a desire whose existence we're not always aware of. She is more my desire than what I'd believed my desire to be; she responds more than I ask, if you will. Because she responds completely.

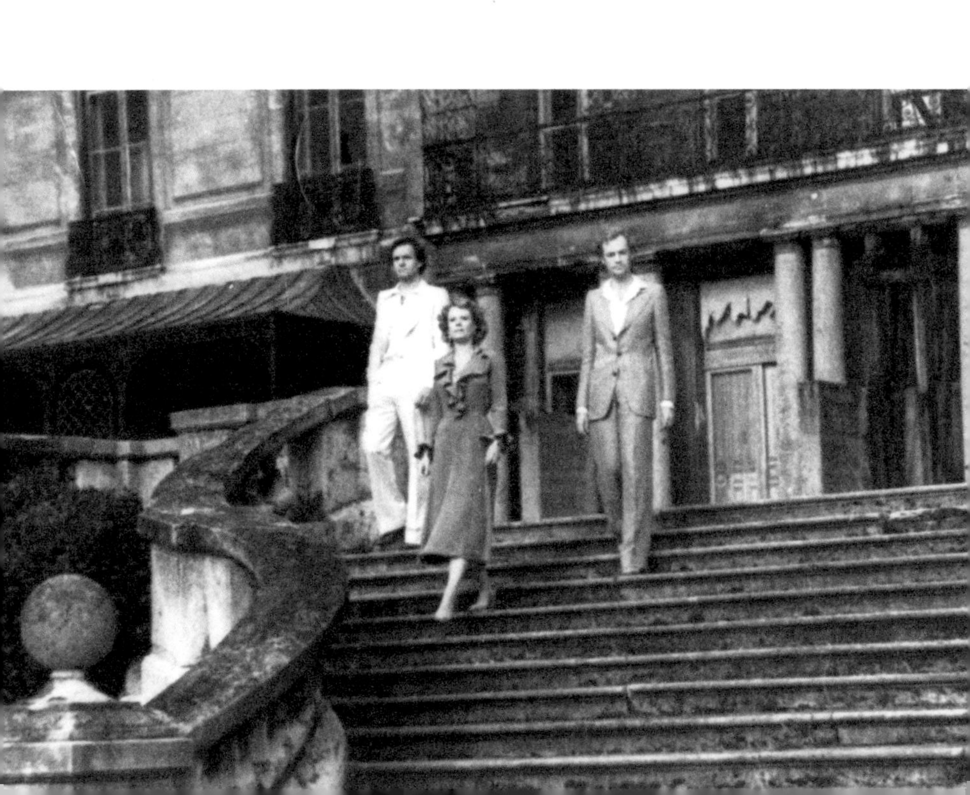

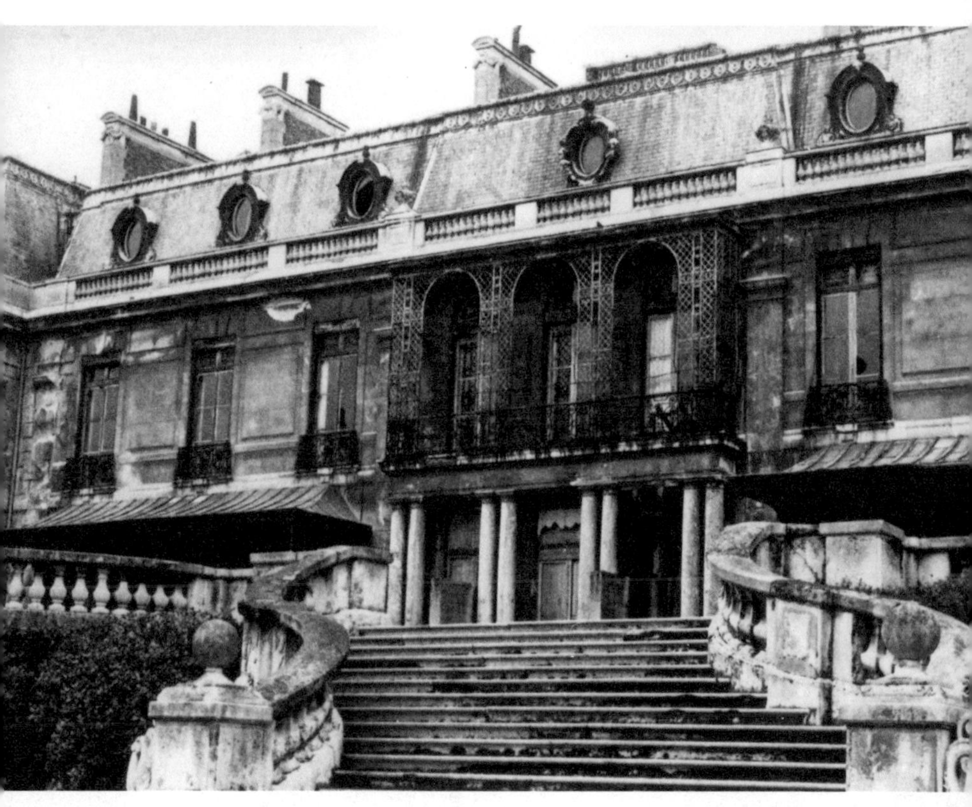

M. D. :

That location left its mark on the entire filming of *India Song*. If Delphine Seyrig did not so much play the role of Anne-Marie Stretter as stand in for her, it's because of the location. The discrepancy between this embassy and a plausible-looking embassy, as you'd see in mainstream film. That hiatus left its mark on the whole film. It is there throughout the film. I think it's the end of the world, yes, I think it's also a film about the end of the world. I think that in *India Song*, it's the end of the world.

M. P. :

Do you mean the end of a certain world, the death throes of a certain society, or more?

M. D. :

More. I'm saying that the end of the world will come when nothing is left on earth but the two monolithic blocs of Russia and America looking at each other in the middle of a desert. That the end corresponds to the monumental idiocy this represents, you understand? What will there be left to do then? I'm thinking about our disappearance, the disappearance of Europe. It's not only the death of history that is written in *India Song*, spoken of in *India Song*, it's the death of our history. My instant attachment to the Château Rothschild was such that I'd have been unable to film in any other place. I'd have sooner given up on the film than to give up that location. This immediate attachment cannot be explained simply in terms of having found a place to shoot a film of fiction. Something else was speaking to me. I'd found a place to tell the story of the end of the world. Colonialism is a detail here—colonialism, leprosy, hunger too. I think that here leprosy has spread, hunger too. Hunger is also yet to come, and, you see, in *India Song*, it arrives.

Death is everywhere in *India Song*. Everywhere—in the setting sun, in the light. It's always evening, always night, in terms of the forms, and the reception, which is perpetually dying. The part of Anne-Marie Stretter that dies is what is incidental in herself, you see, and I think that in death she will still be here, completely present. And I think it is conceivable that another woman will come and take over from her. Apart from the magic of the name, she'd play the same role. Still, I can't yet conceive of another Anne-Marie Stretter. Just as when you are coming out of one love, you cannot enter another, just like that—it isn't possible.

M. P. :

And when Anne-Marie Stretter commits suicide? Does she commit suicide in the sea?

M. D. :

Yes, but I don't know whether it's suicide. It's as if she becomes part of the Indian Ocean, a sort of matricial sea. Something comes full circle with her death. There's nothing else that she can do. I think it's a completely logical suicide. There's nothing tragic about it. She can't live anywhere else but there, and she lives off this place, she lives off the despair secreted every day by India, by Calcutta, and she dies of it. She dies as if she has been poisoned by India. She could kill herself some other way, but no, she kills herself in the water, yes, in the Indian Ocean.

What is this? A customs wharf from over there, the
Ganges Mesopotamia, lost here, in S. Thala?

These residential villas, closed, white – those of
the English quarter of Calcutta?

These clouds - a monsoon advancing, a floating
continent, to go die over Nepal?

That's it: *over there* has moved. It's here now. We
have entered the place bereft of love.

(La femme du Gange)

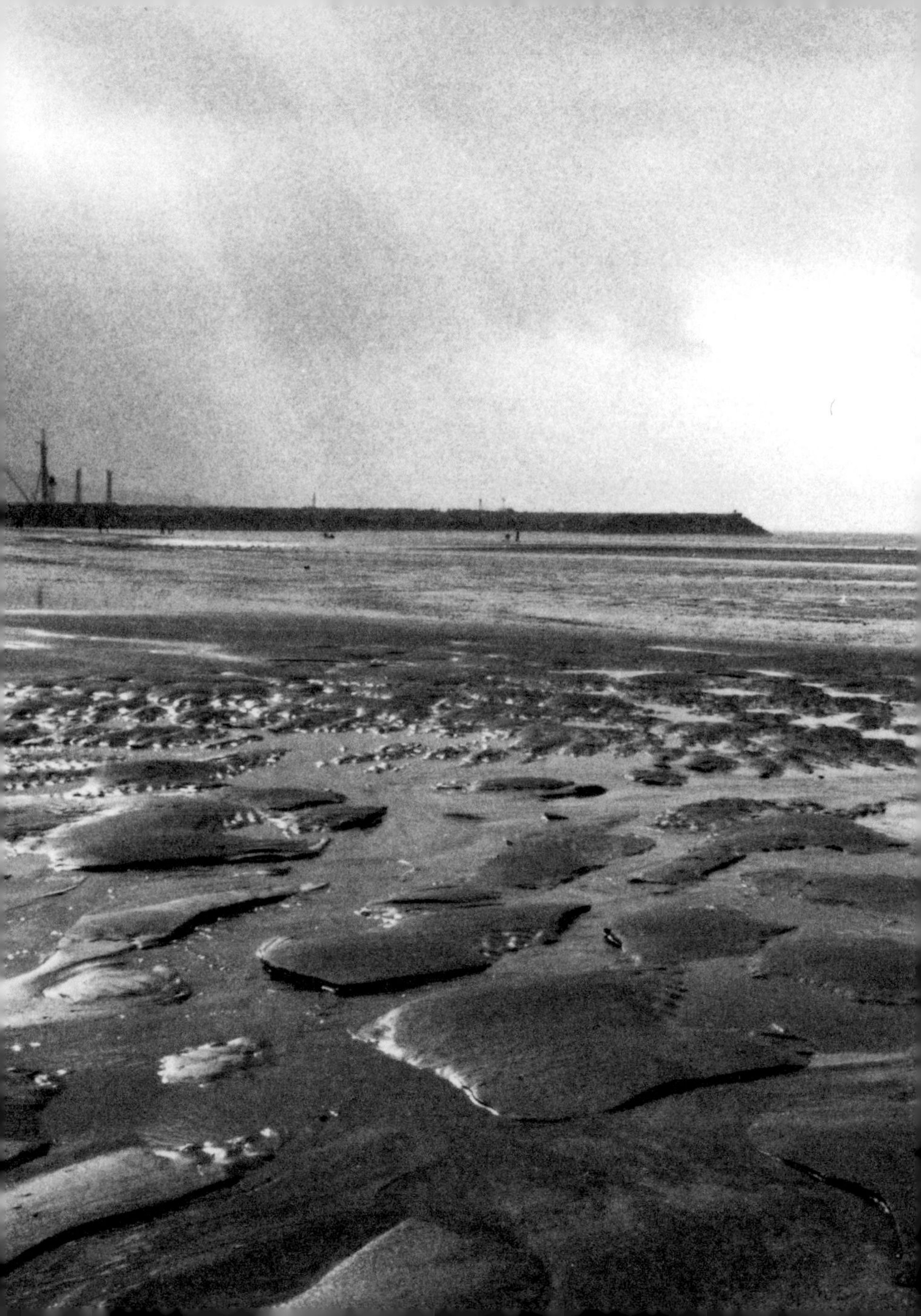

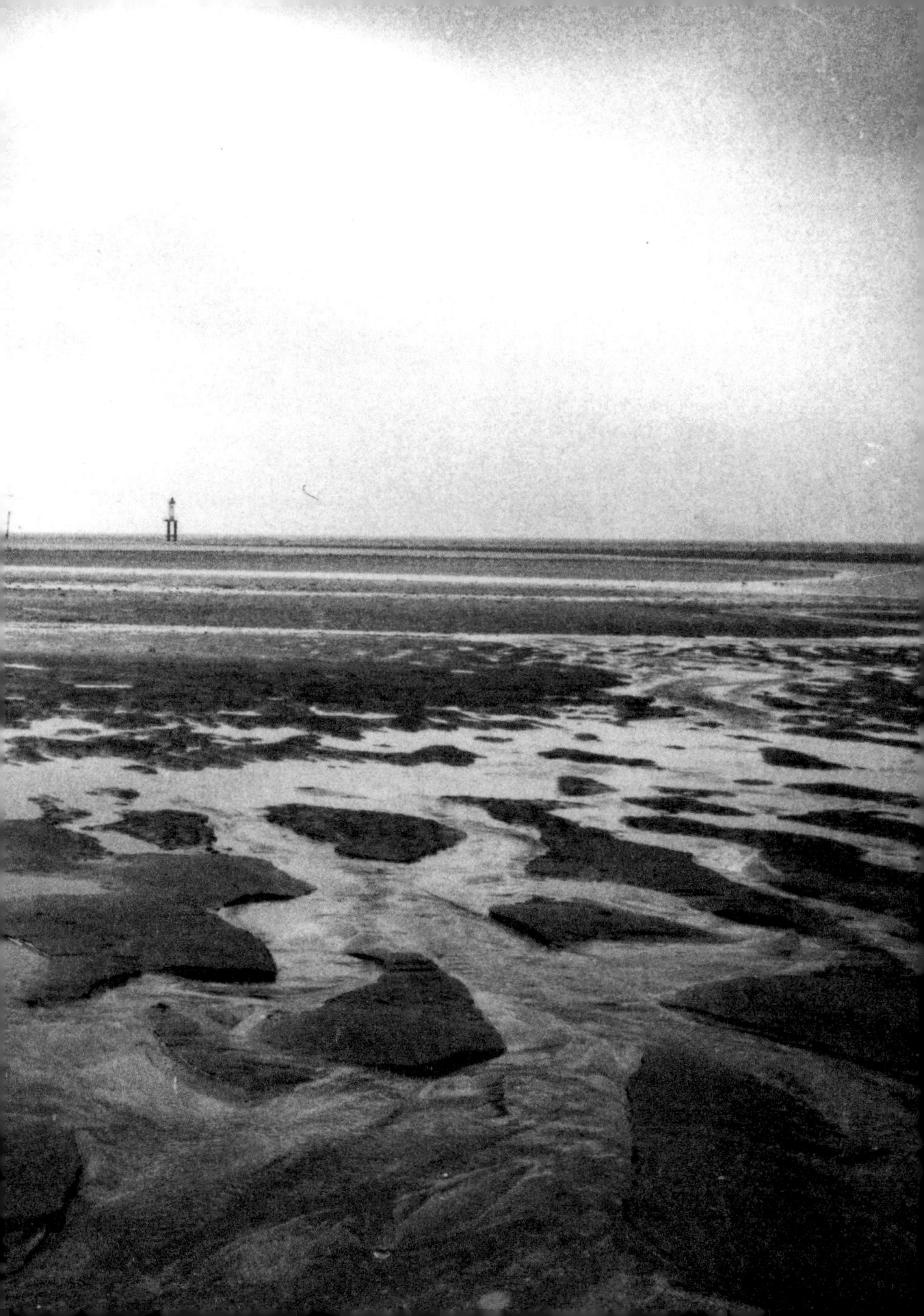

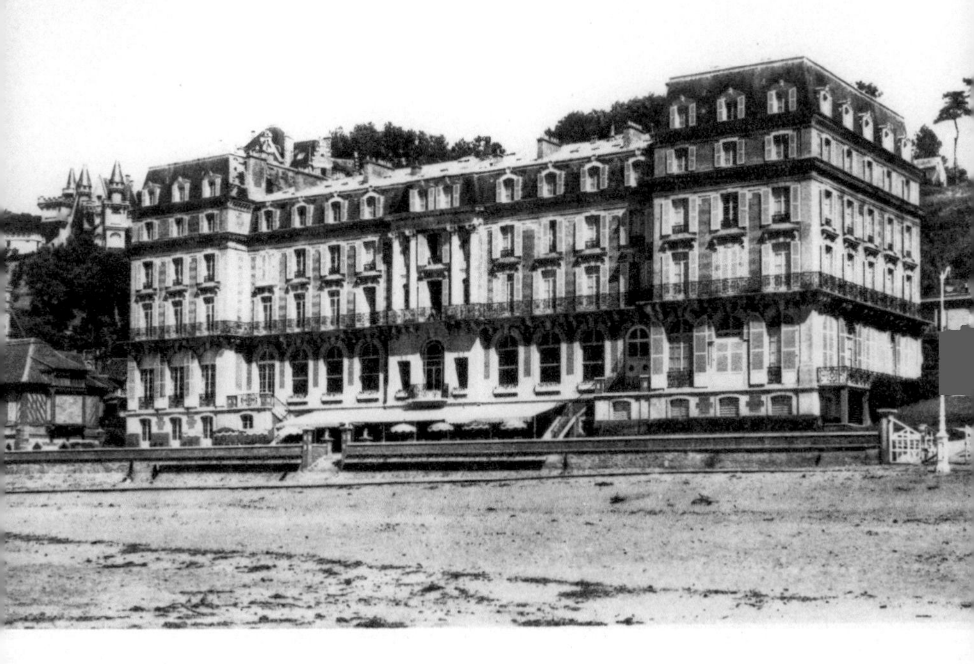

M. D. :

I wrote Lol V. Stein here, in this building, but it was only later that this place where I wrote the book became a place in the book. I mean that *L'Amour,* which is part of *The Ravishing of Lol V. Stein*, took place here.

I ask myself whether the sand and the beach, rather than the sea, are not the setting of S. Thala. The tides we have here are magnificent. At low tide, there are three kilometres of beach, entire lands, countries of sand, completely interchangeable. The country of no one, you understand, nameless.

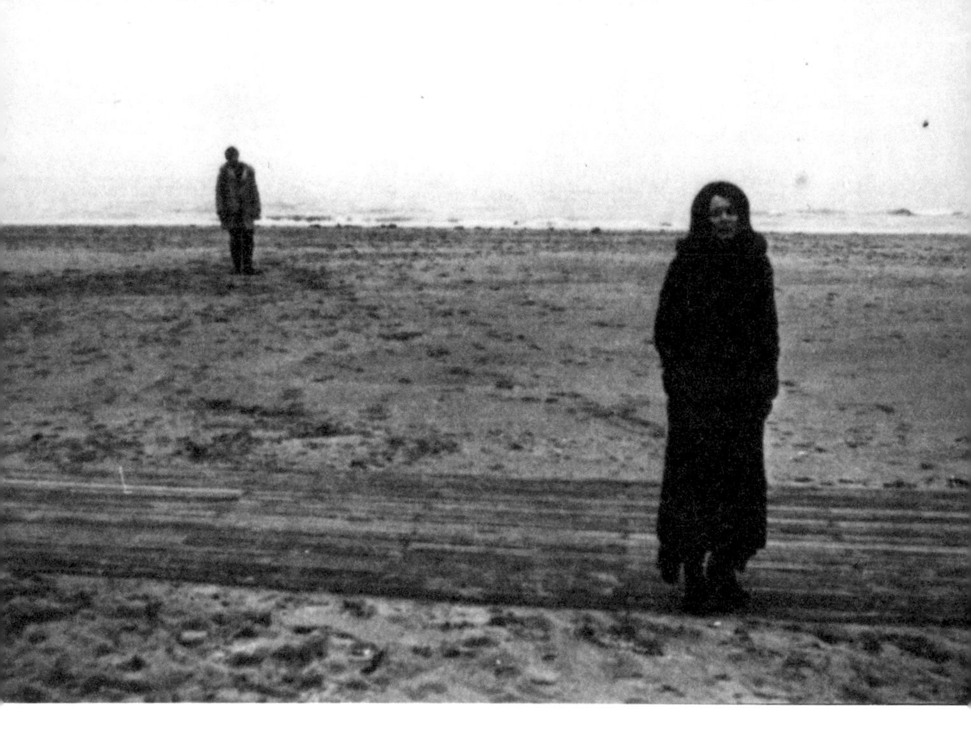

The Traveller:
Where are we?
The Woman:
Here, it is S. Thala, until the river.
The Traveller:
And after the river?
The Woman :
After the river, it's still S. Thala.

(La femme du Gange)

87

M. D. :
So the material is uniform. I think it's the sand, and the people in *La femme du Gange* live on the sand. They walk there, all day, on the sand, and all night. It's the total nullification of habitat. They do not inhabit. Their wandering over the sand is a kind of pure, animal wandering.

In my books I've always been by the sea—I was thinking that just now. My relation with the sea started very early, when my mother bought the dam and the land in *Barrage contre le Pacifique*, and the sea swallowed everything, and we were ruined. The sea terrifies me. It's the thing I'm most afraid of in the world… My nightmares, my dreams of horror always have to do with the tide, with being swallowed up by sea water.

All the different places in Lol V. Stein are places by the sea. She is always near the sea. For a long time I saw very white cities— bleached by salt like that, almost as if they were totally covered in salt—on the roads and in the places where Lola Valérie Stein goes. And it was later that I understood that these were not just places by the sea, but that they were connected to a northern sea that was also the sea of my childhood… limitless seas.

M. P. :

And the name S. Thala?

M. D. :

(*Smiling.*) It was very late, yes, much later that I realized it wasn't S. Thala, but Thalassa.

M. P. :

That wasn't your intention when you wrote it?

M. D. :

No, absolutely not. But you know, I did *Hiroshima, mon amour*, sixteen… sixteen years ago now—and I realized only two years ago, perhaps, that the meaning I was giving to Nevers, the French city of Nevers, was that of "never," the English word for *jamais*. I often play tricks on myself like that, it's strange. In *L'Amante anglaise*, I'm always talking about plants, the plants that grow in the sand, on the sand islands, where there are sheep, you know, and I realized very recently about this sand— that madwoman in *L'Amante anglaise* always talks about sand, well, the sand is time… It gives me such pleasure when I discover these things that were unintentional, these accidents, if you like.

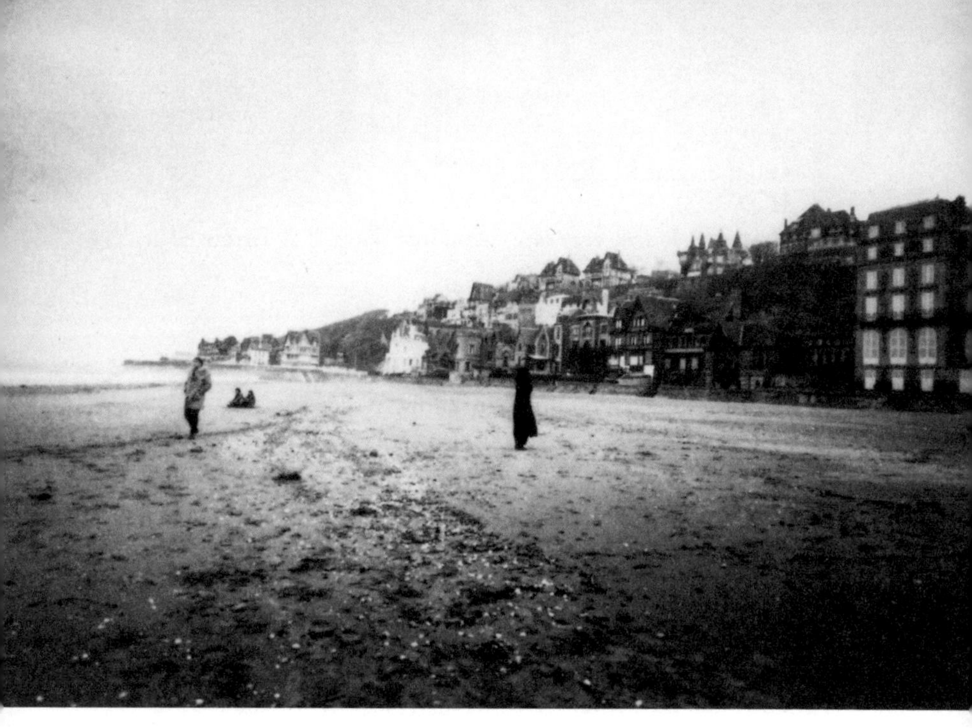

M. P. :

The sea is omnipresent in *La femme du Gange*, it's like the breath of the film.

M. D. :

Yes, they're by the sea, walking, moving along in time with the sea. Their movements are the movements of the tides. The city is opposite, and it appears to them monolithic, one solid block. They're not bored. They walk in a way that expresses interest. Their gaze is pure, unadulterated, with no point of comparison.

To look at the sea is to look at everything. And to look at the sand is to look at everything, at a whole.

M. P. :

So it's a little like the sea, constant movement? When the film ends, the film could continue—I mean, does the film continue?

M. D. :

Yes… But it also began before the film. They've been there for a very long time when the film begins, and they're still there… Well, they're still there now, anyway for me, though the film has ended. When I think of *La femme du Gange*, they are there, they're still there, walking, walking incessantly, making their way across the expanses of sand.

The story. It begins.

Began before the walk along the edge of the sea, the cry, the gesture, the movement of the sea, the movement of the light.

But now it becomes visible.

It is already tracing it-self onto on the sand, on the sea.

(L'Amour)

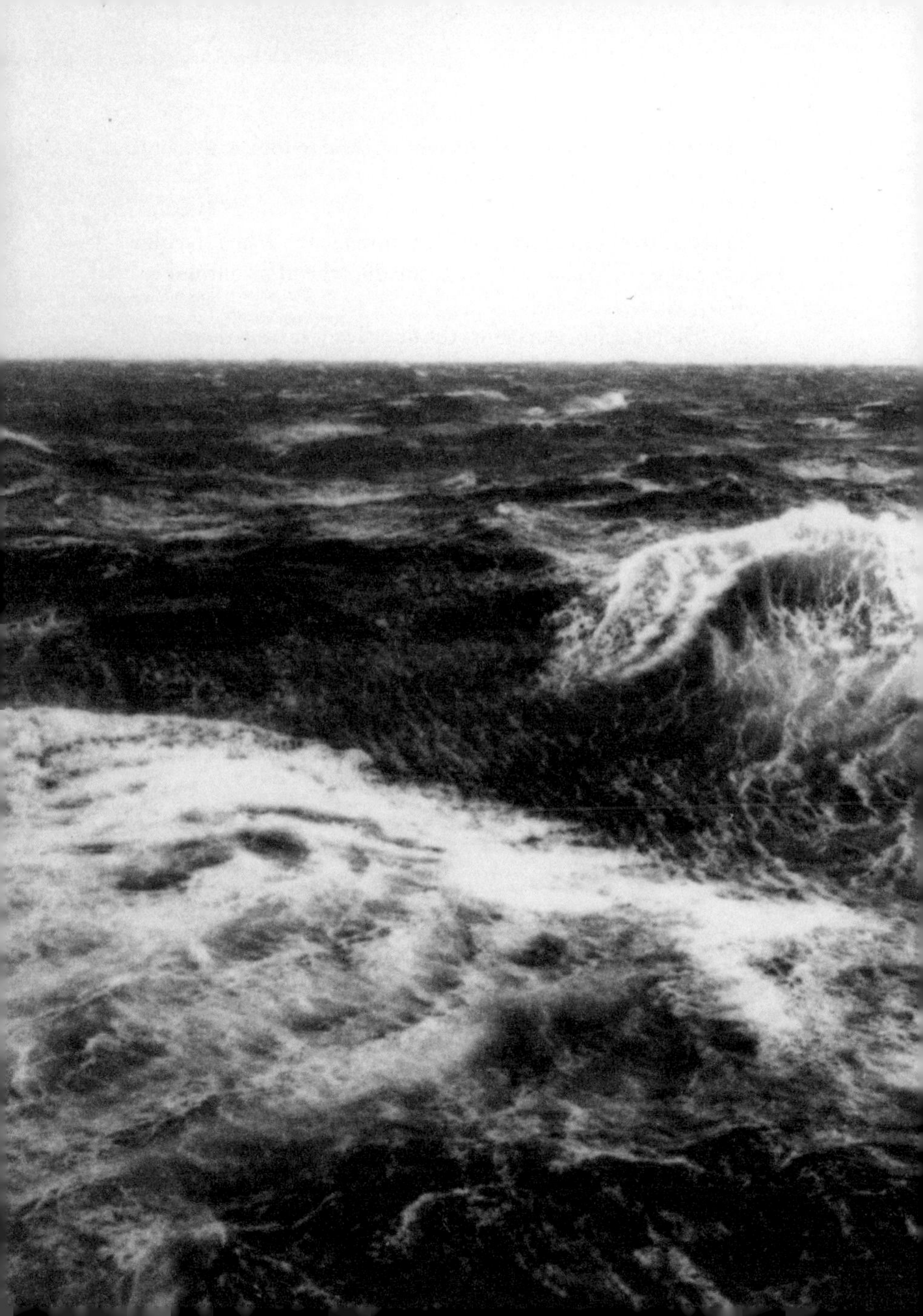

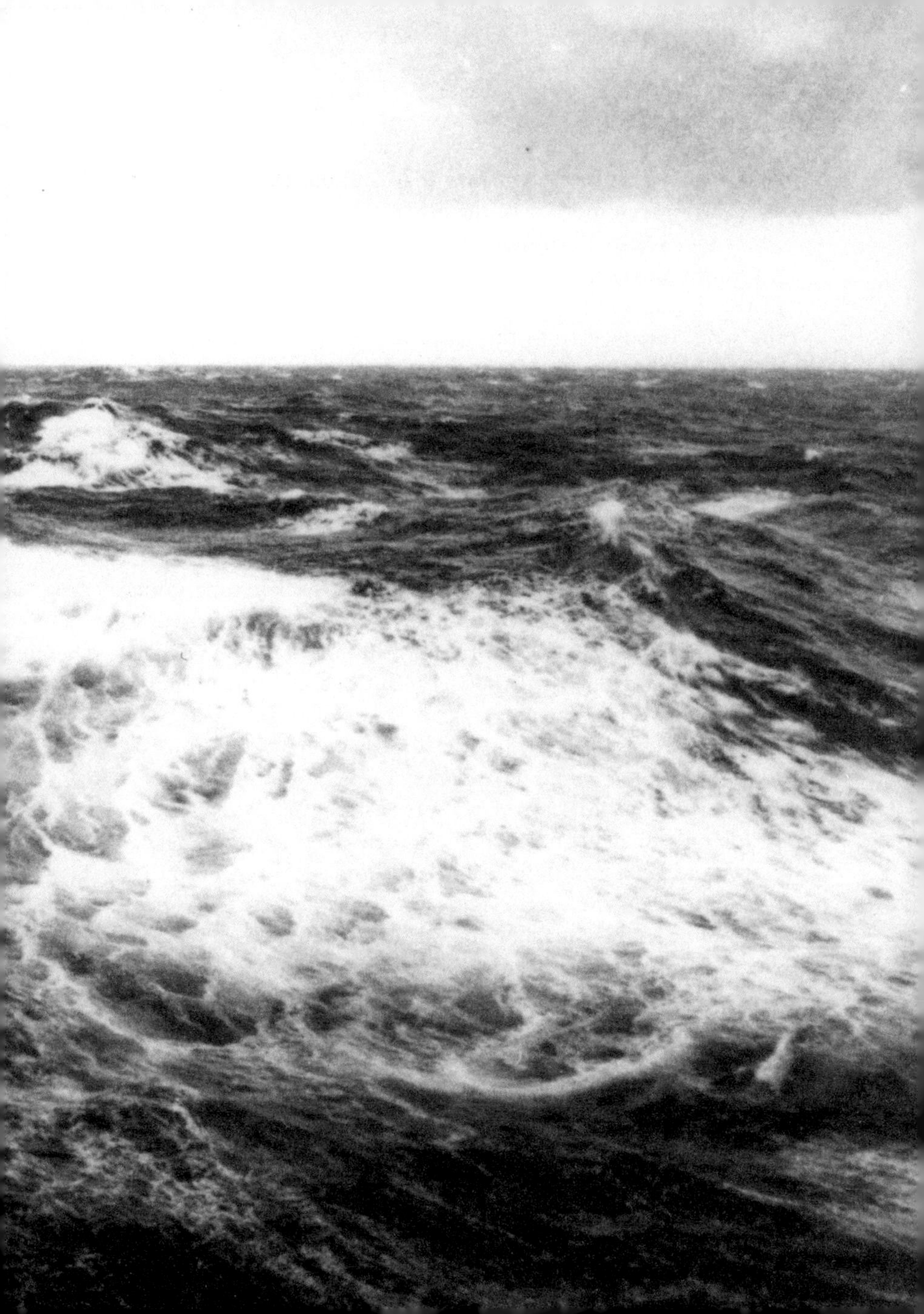

M. D. :

La femme du Gange is a film that counted enormously for me. Maybe even more than the others, maybe even more than *India Song* because I think that *India Song* was already there in *La femme du Gange*, waiting to be found. That is, it was there inside of *La Femme du Gange*, but it had to be pulled out of the sand, removed from the sand. But it was there. Whereas with *La femme du Gange*... I don't think there was anything there before—anyway, not inside of me, you understand. I sometimes have the impression that I started writing with *Le ravissement de Lol V. Stein,* with *L'Amour,* and *La Femme du Gange*, but that the writing, the full breadth of the writing, was attained with the film. That *Lol V. Stein* was an instance of writing, as was *L'Amour,* but that in *La Femme du Gange,* everything was mixed together, as if I'd gone back in time, gone back to a place before writing. I was mad when I was editing *La Femme du Gange.* When I found the voices for *La Femme du Gange* I was mad with anxiety. But perhaps this place of mad anxiety is my place.

It was also as if everything had already been written, and *La Femme du Gange* were a written text but had to be deciphered. Whereas the walking by the sea was written, that was written, I took only one part of it when I actually wrote *La Femme du Gange* and *L'Amour.* In the film, everything is written, even the moments when they are walking in silence are written. They may not be legible, but they are written. Whereas, in the actual writing, only a part of what is written comes through. It's as if it were only possible to write completely by going beyond language, of course, or beyond writing in the strict sense. For me, the sea has the form of writing. It's like pages, you understand, pages full of writing, empty by dint of being full, illegible by dint of having been written upon—of being full of writing.

In short, yes, it raises the question of cinema, of the image. We're always inundated, aren't we, by the written word and language when we transpose things into writing. It's impossible to convey everything, to take account of everything, whereas with the image, you are writing completely. All of filmic space is written, it's one hundred times the space of the book. But I discovered this only with *La Femme du Gange*, not with the other films.

M. P. :

Not before *La Femme du Gange* ?

M. D. :

No. Not even with *Hiroshima, mon amour,* which apparently is very written, almost chatty, you see. Yes, *Hiroshima* is quite talkative.

La Femme du Gange, no. The written word is not talkative. What's talkative is the spoken word. The written word, never. But ninety percent of books are made up of the spoken word. And you really feel that threshold when you move from certain books and from certain films to others.

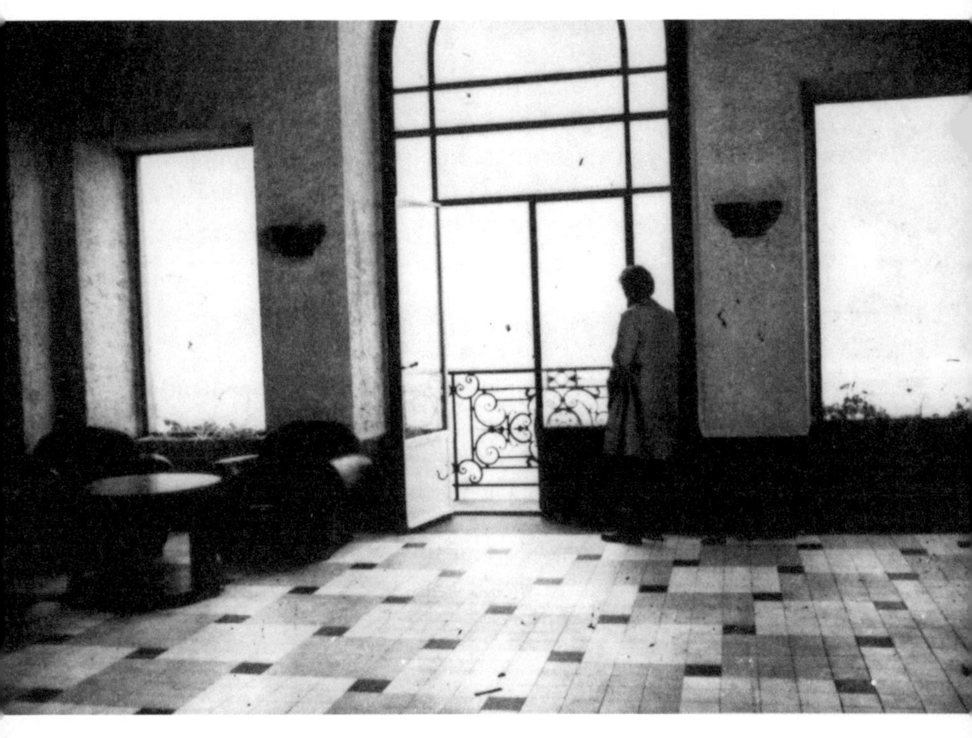

The Traveller, seen from behind, stares out towards a point in the sand. The murmur of the sea caught between the walls echoes.

Voice 1 :
Me too, sometimes another memory comes to me.
(Silence.)

Voice 2 :
It seems as if there are people there.
Voice 1 :
No...it's only the sand...the sea...
It's nothing...
(Silence.)

Voice 1 :
Today, the air smells of salt, iodine...Don't you think so?
Voice 2 :
Yes.
Voice 1 :
What impossible, terrible desire... What love.
The Traveller is still looking.
Voice 1 :
Do you still want to die?
Voice 2 :
Yes.
And then I forget.
I look.

(La femme du Gange)

M. D. :

In my cinema, of course, I make no movements. Nor in my books. In my books there are fewer and fewer stylistic movements, I remain in the same place. I write and film in the same place. And when I go to another place, it's the same place. I can explain it to myself when it comes to my films. There are many things I can explain about film, but none at all when it comes to writing, you see. Or rather things to do with writing remain very obscure to me. With film, because I feel a kind of disgust for the films that have been made, at least for most of the films that have been made, I'd like to start from nothing, with a very primitive grammar… very simple, very primal, almost. No movement, start all over.

In any case, the films I make come from the same place as my books. It's what I call the place of passion—a place where we are deaf and blind. Anyway, I try to be there as much as possible. Whereas the kind of cinema that is made for diversion, for entertainment—the kind of film, what to call it, I call it Saturday cinema, or the cinema of consumer society—is made in the place of the spectator, and according to very precise recipes, designed to entertain and to maintain a hold on the spectator for the duration of the show. Once the show is over, this kind of film leaves nothing behind, nothing. It's a kind of cinema that erases itself as soon as the film is over. I get the feeling that my films begin the day after they've been seen, the same as with a book one reads.

The sea, flat - Daytime, but gray.

The madman: He's there, he was walking, he is walking, he hasn't plunged into the light of India. He has not ceased, in perfect bewilderment, to be in S. Thala. With him, the film begins again, here, in S. Thala.

Voice 1:
What's he doing?
Voice 2:
You know, guarding.
Voice 1:
The sea?
Voice 2, hesitation:
No...
Voice 1:
The movement of light?
Voice 2:
No...
Voice 1:
The movement of water?
Voice 2:
No...
Voice 1:
Memory...?
Voice 2:
Ah, maybe... maybe...

(La femme du Gange)

M. D. :

That's it, he is guarding memory, yes. He has no memory and he is guarding memory, yes. He is mad. He says: "I'm mad." "Me, I'm mad," he says: "The others are this or that, and me, what I am is mad, I'm mad." There's an equivalence.

M. P. :

I'm thinking of the scene where the madman dances in the hall… In the script for *La femme du Ganges*, you write: "The first bar of the S. Thala song comes out of his mouth. It starts again. This first bar is heard several times. The memory of everyone passes through the madman, through the madman's hollow form. The sieve-head through which the memory of everything passes is incorporated into the walls here."

M. D. :

A sieve-head, yes, full of holes. That's it, yes. Because he is nothing and offers no resistance to anything, and because memory, for me, is something that is spread across all places. Because I perceive places in that way…

M. P. :

As containers for history?

M. D. :

Yes. For example, it's very rare for me to take a walk in my garden in the country, or here on the beach, without reliving certain things that are very, well, immeasurably distant. They come to me in flashes, just like that. And I tell myself that it's the places themselves that harbour memory… and that if we didn't put up cultural or social resistance, you see, we'd have the permeability to receive it. The madman is porous. He is nothing, so things pass right through him. So the story of S. Thala passes through him. The story of Lol V. Stein, which is the story of S. Thala. They are one and the same.

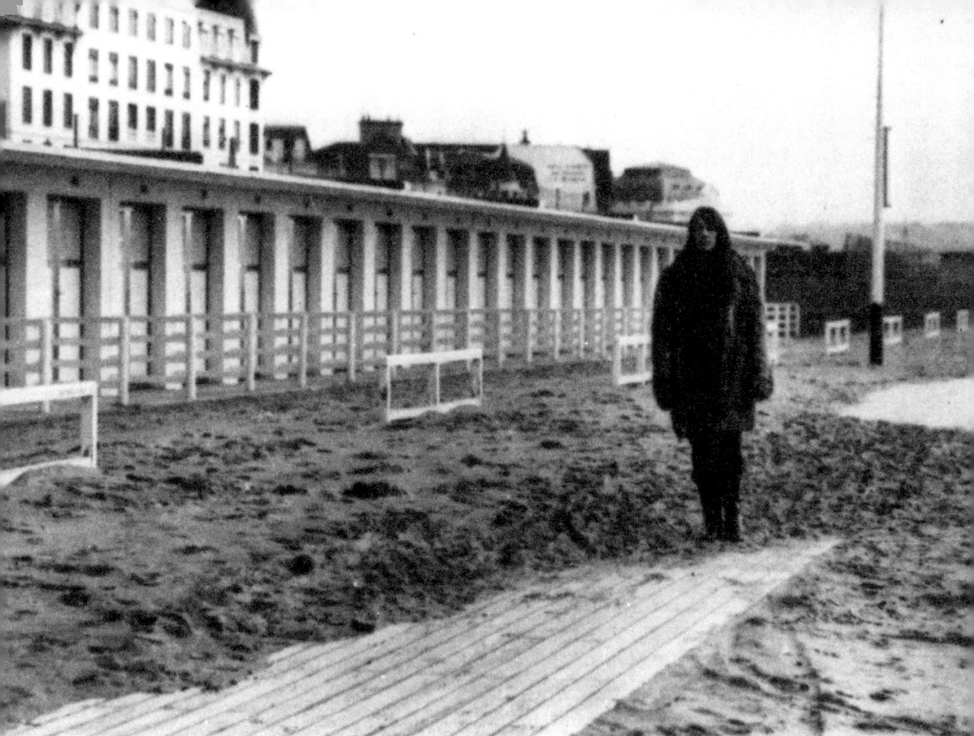

"S. Thala.
They walk. They walk into S. Thala. She walks straight, facing the wind, between the walls.
The traveller says:
— Eighteen years. [He pauses] That's how old you were.
— It was your age.
She lifts her eyes, looks out at the petrified land-scape.
She says:
— I don't know anymore."

(L'Amour)

M. P. :

When Lol returns ten years after the ball of S. Thala, she walks on the beach, like the characters in *La femme du Gange*…

M. D. :

We're in a totally corporeal world. It's while she's walking that one memory comes to her and another memory leaves her, and the transfer takes place.

M. P. :

Yes…

M. D. :

It doesn't happen through reflection, though. You see, Lol V. Stein is unable to reflect. She stopped living before the onset of reflection. Maybe that is why she's so dear to me, I mean, so close, or I don't know… Reflection is a time that I find… suspect. It bores me. And if you look at my characters, they are all, they are all from before that time. I mean the characters I love, the ones I love deeply.

This is undoubtedly the state I'm trying to reach when I'm writing—a state of listening that's extremely intense, you understand, but from the outside. When people who write say, when you're writing, you're in a state of great concentration, I say, no, when I'm writing I have a sense of being in a state of extreme loss of concentration. I am no longer in possession of myself at all, I am myself a sieve. I have holes in my head. That is the only way I can explain what I write because there are things I don't recognize in what I write. So they come from quite another place. I'm not alone in writing when I write. But I know that. It's presumptuous to believe you're alone in front of the page, while things are coming at you from all sides. Obviously, it's not the same every time. Things come to you from near or far, they come from yourself, they come from someone else, but none of this matters, they come to you from some external place.

What lands on you when you're writing is undoubtedly the mass of your experience, so to speak, quite simply… quite simply… But this mass of uncatalogued and unrationalized experience is in a state of primal disorder. We are haunted by our experience. We have to let it do what it will do. Lol V. Stein is a person who is completely haunted by the experience of S. Thala, by the ball. It's an ugly word, "experience," but I don't know what other word to use.

But she's haunted, in the way a place is haunted.

She can't make compromises with remembering, she is crushed by remembering, and it starts all over every day. Every day of her life regains its freshness, a kind of primal freshness. That is Lol V. Stein, a person who remembers everything for the first time every day. And every day it's repeated, she remembers everything for the first time every day, as if between each day in the life of Lol V. Stein there were unfathomable chasms of forgetting. She never gets used to memory. Or to forgetting, for that matter. But she is still very, very deeply embedded in the written word. I've never seen Lol V. Stein… really… you know. She's a bit like a person who has drowned and suddenly rises to the surface of the water, and then sinks back down again. That's how I see Lol V. Stein, she appears at the surface of the water and sinks again. I'll probably die without knowing exactly who she is. Usually, when I write a book, I know more or less what I've done. I'm still in some sense its reader… But with this book, no. When I did Lol V. Stein, it completely eluded me.

Of course, I can show Lol V. Stein in a film, but I can only show her hidden, when she's like a dead dog on the beach, covered in sand, you understand…

M. P. :
In *La femme du Gange*…
M. D. :
It's in *La femme du Gange*, yes, I'm confused… Yes, she's waiting outside the casino, she's lying on the beach half dead, her fingers half buried, she's got a bag beside her that looks like a young girl's bag, it seems to me, she's dressed all in white, half dead, asleep—in that case, I see her, then I see her. But alive… I see what she sees, I see her husband, I see her children, I see her, I see her. I see her husband, I see her children, I see her cities, the cities where she trails about, I see her friends, I see her houses very well, the walls, the gardens, the lanes, I see all that, but her face when I see it, I don't see it.

M. P. :
So if you made a film of Lol V. Stein, of the scene at the ball, you wouldn't show her?

M. D. :
No, I would. I'd show her, her, but destroyed, already filmed; she's still sunk inside of the book, she hasn't emerged from it but she's still damaged by comments and readings. I mean, it's a book that's been translated all over, so it has trailed through many hands, many minds. Lol V. Stein is already a sort of prostitution. But Lol V. Stein when she emerged, after she came out of me and I saw her for the first time, after seeing her for the first time, I'd never really see her again. Lol V. Stein belongs to you, she belongs to others… and when she goes back in time to the ball of S. Thala, to the moment of her birth, she is already battered and bruised like a whore. I can see her all made up, bejeweled, and collapsing under it all, under the makeup and the jewels. It's strange, but I no longer know the person who came out of here eight or nine

years ago. I can't claim to see her, so I won't make a film, or I'll make it with the tatters, the remains of Lol V. Stein. I can work on Lol V. Stein with those things alone. There's no sense to be got from her, Lol V. Stein signifies nothing. Lol V. Stein is what you make of her, she has no existence other than that. I think I've just said something about her. She had meaning for me, she signified something, when she came out, or rather when I stumbled across her—I can't say "came out of me," I never talk like that, but I can say that afterwards she belonged to anyone who wanted her. That sounds familiar, yes.

M. P. :

Like Anne-Marie Stretter, who belongs to anyone who wants her, who is anybody's woman.

M. D. :

Yes, it's my sort of prostitution.

M. P. :

But it has to do with desire.

M. D. :

Ah, yes, absolutely. That's what the book was about, yes. While I was writing it, there was a time—I think I told you—a time when I was afraid. I'd scream. I think that I'd overcome something, but I don't know what it was… because it's possible to cross a threshold without passing into a clearer form of consciousness, perhaps the threshold is opaque. I fell into even greater opacity after that and that's what made me start to scream, I remember. It had never happened to me before. I was writing, and all of a sudden I could hear that I was screaming because I was afraid. I no longer really know what I was afraid of. That was a learned form of fear, too, a fear of losing my mind, a little…

M. P. :

With the women in your books, I'm thinking of Lol V. Stein, Anne-Marie Stretter, and so on, it's always desire, and…

M. D. :

Women are desire.

M. P. :

Women…

M. D. :

We don't write from the same place as men do. And when women don't write from a place of desire, they aren't writing, they're plagiarizing.

M. P. :

And in *La femme du Gange*, you use two voices that are external to the story and linked through a relationship of desire, as in *India Song*, when the voices from the beginning are also the voices of two women who desire each other…

M. D. :

Yes, but everywhere it's me, I think… the two women. I can't be everywhere at once when I'm writing, yet I want to be inside of everything. I'm not plural, but the voices speak to me everywhere, and I try… I nonetheless try to account for some of that profusion, and for a long time I thought that the voices were external, but I don't think that anymore. I think they are myself, the voices are me if I didn't write, me if I had better understanding, me if I loved women, you see, or if I loved a woman, me if I were dead, if I understood, etc. It's a sort of multiplicity that we all have inside us, men, women, but it has been butchered. In general, we have one meagre voice at most, the one we use for talking. Whereas we should be completely inundated with voices.

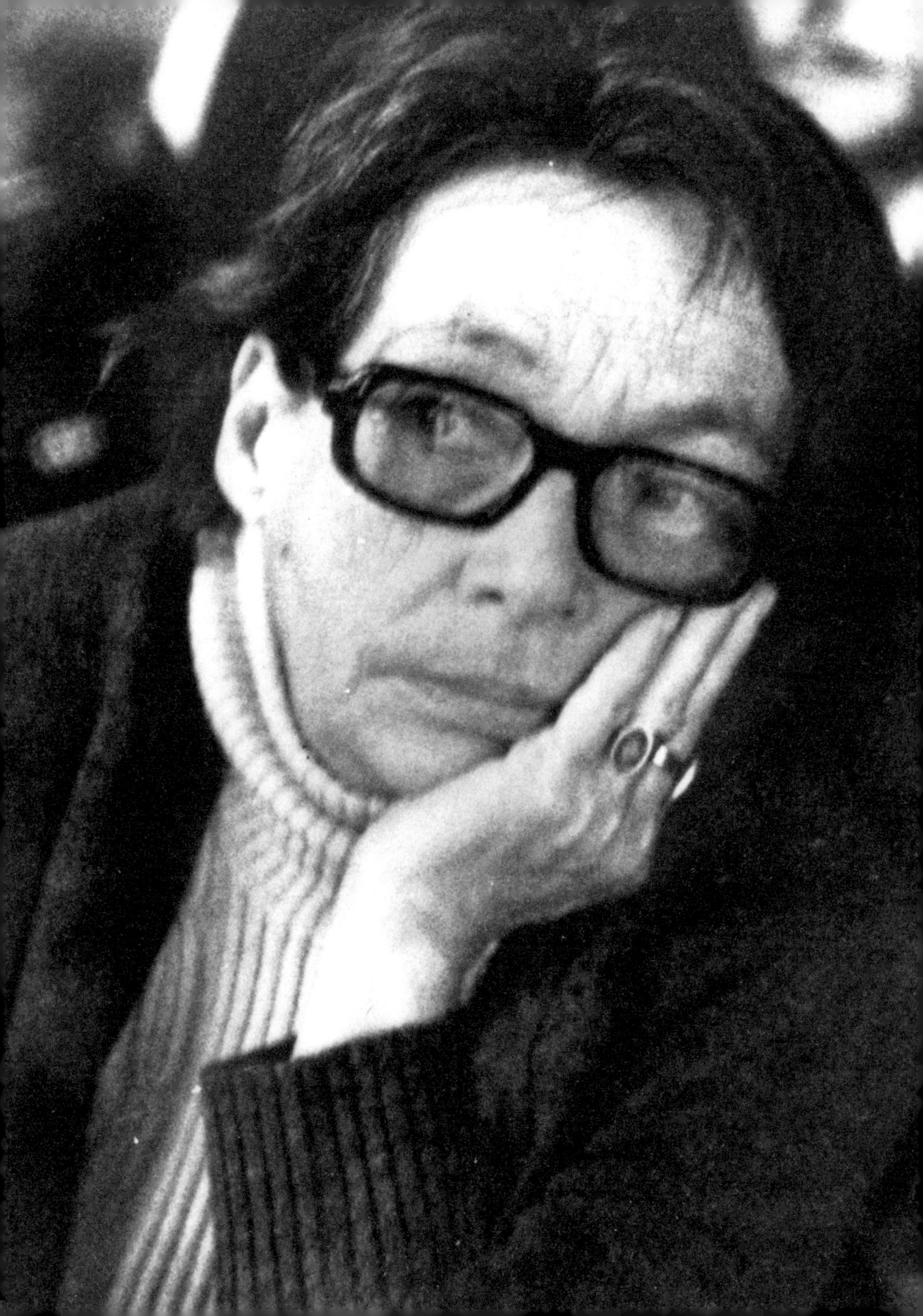

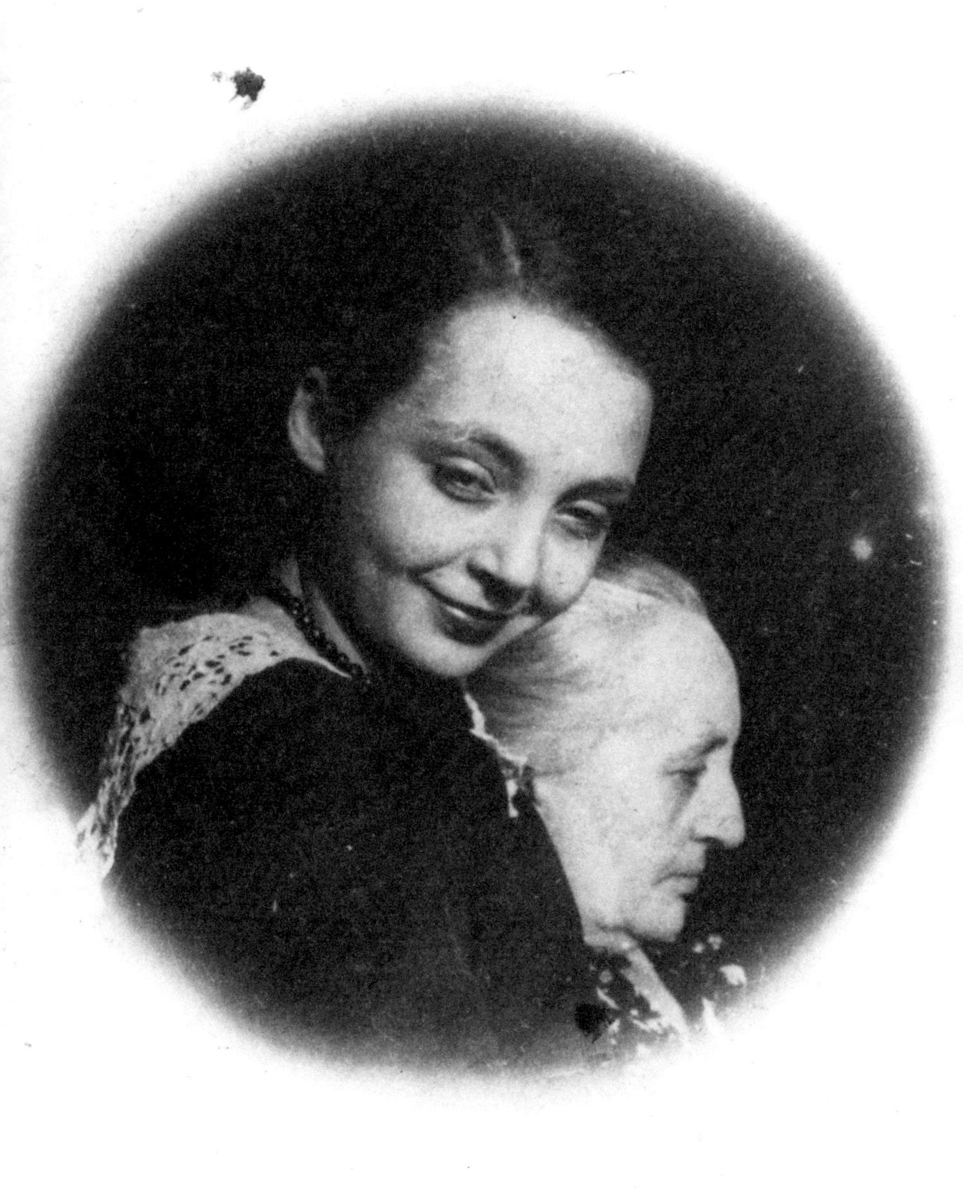

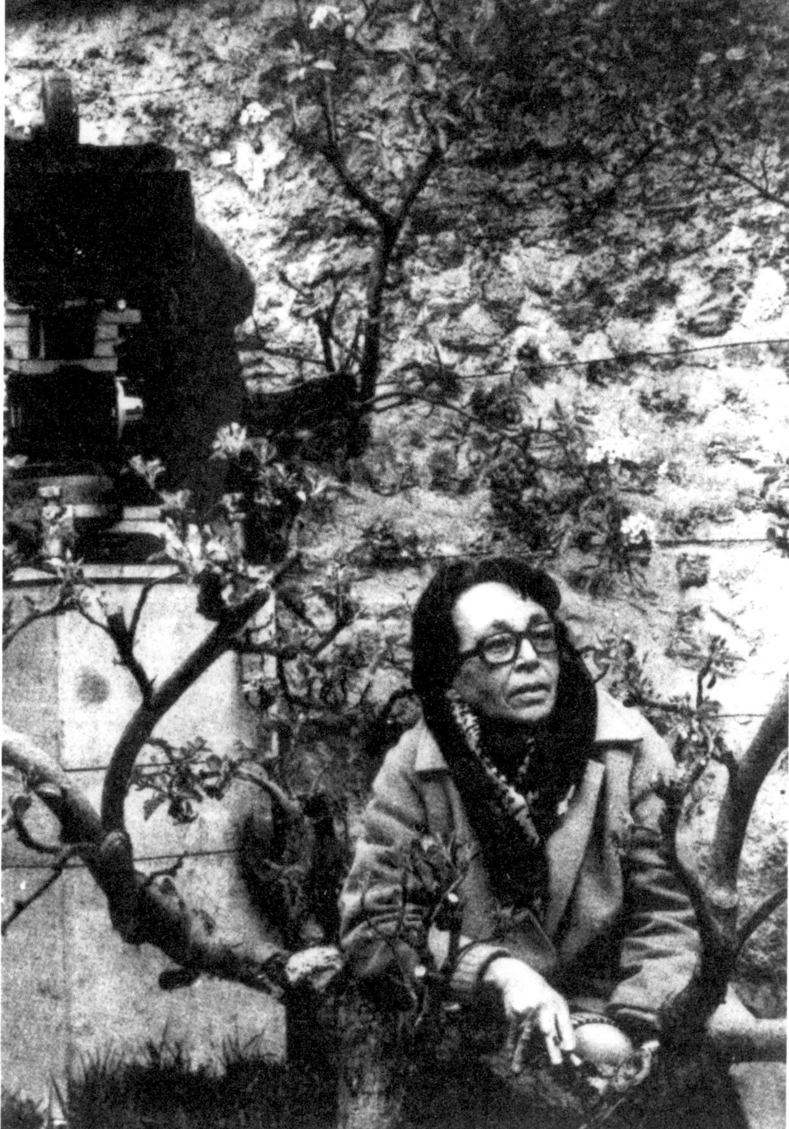

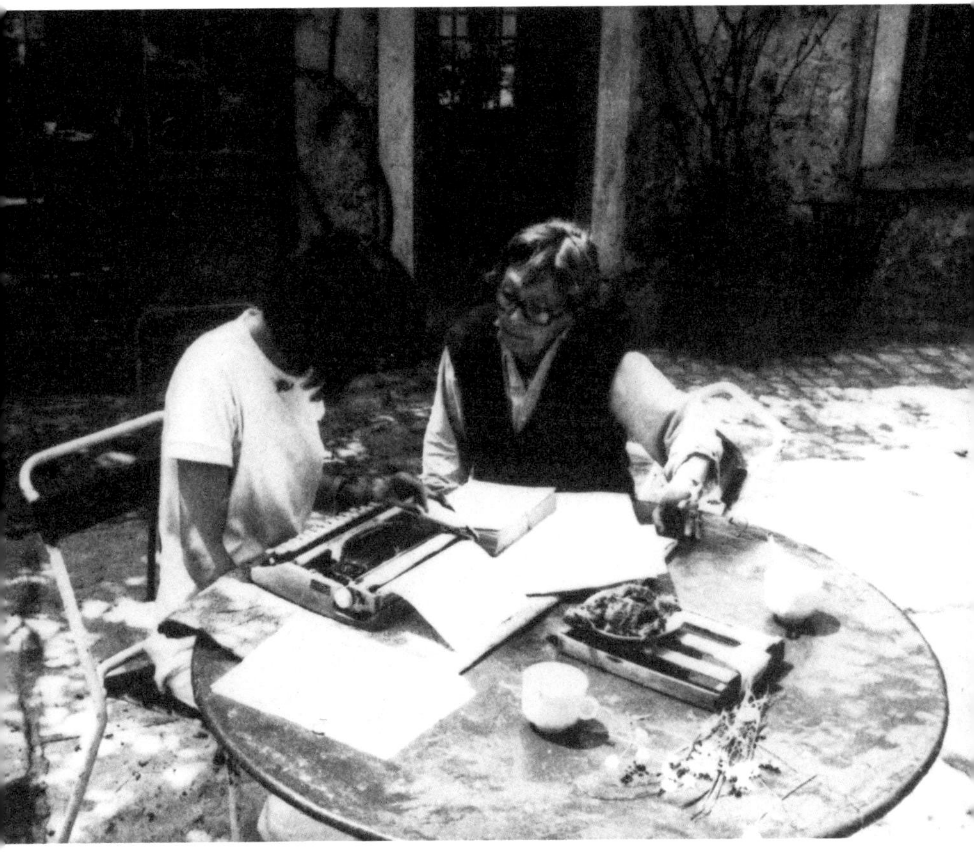

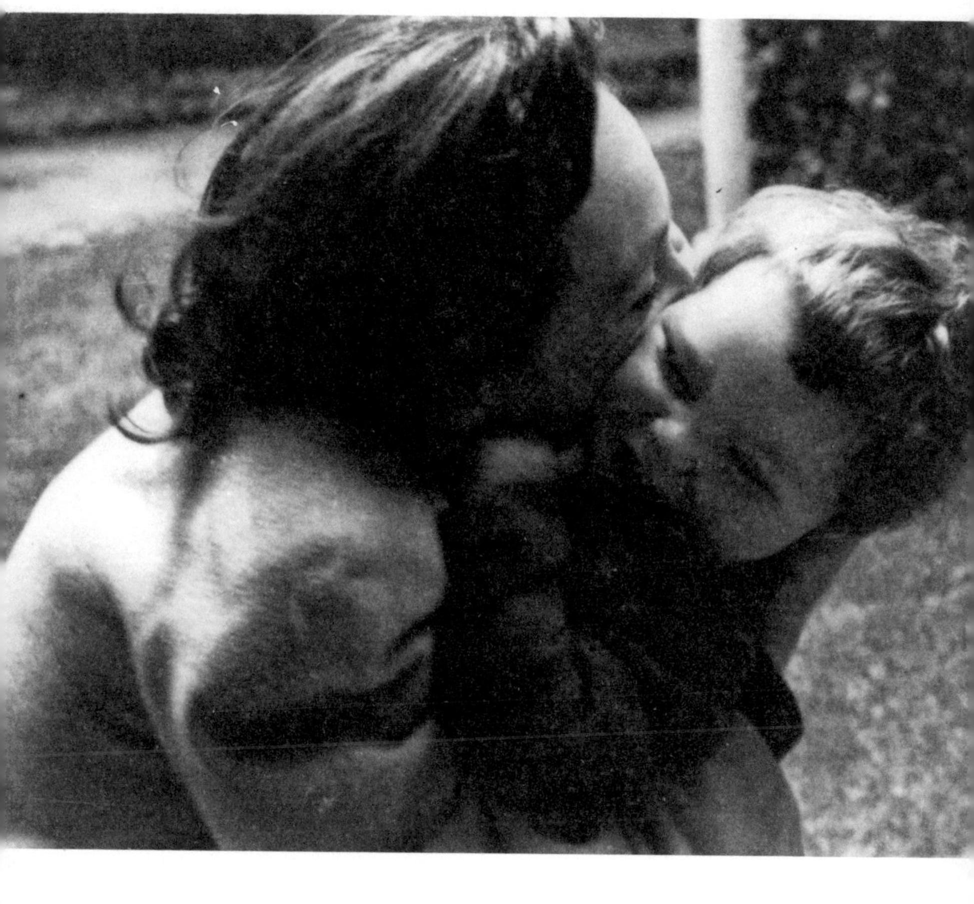

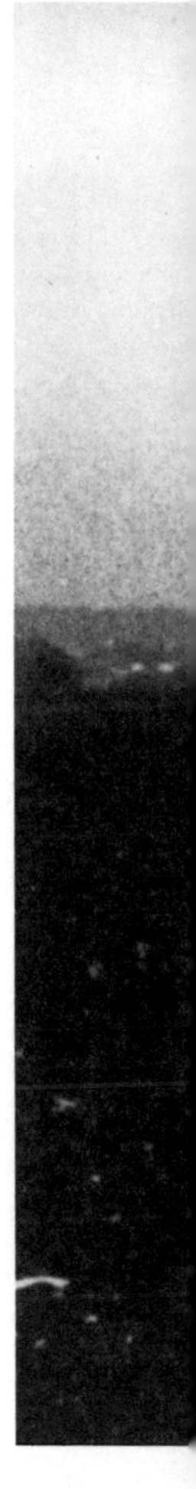

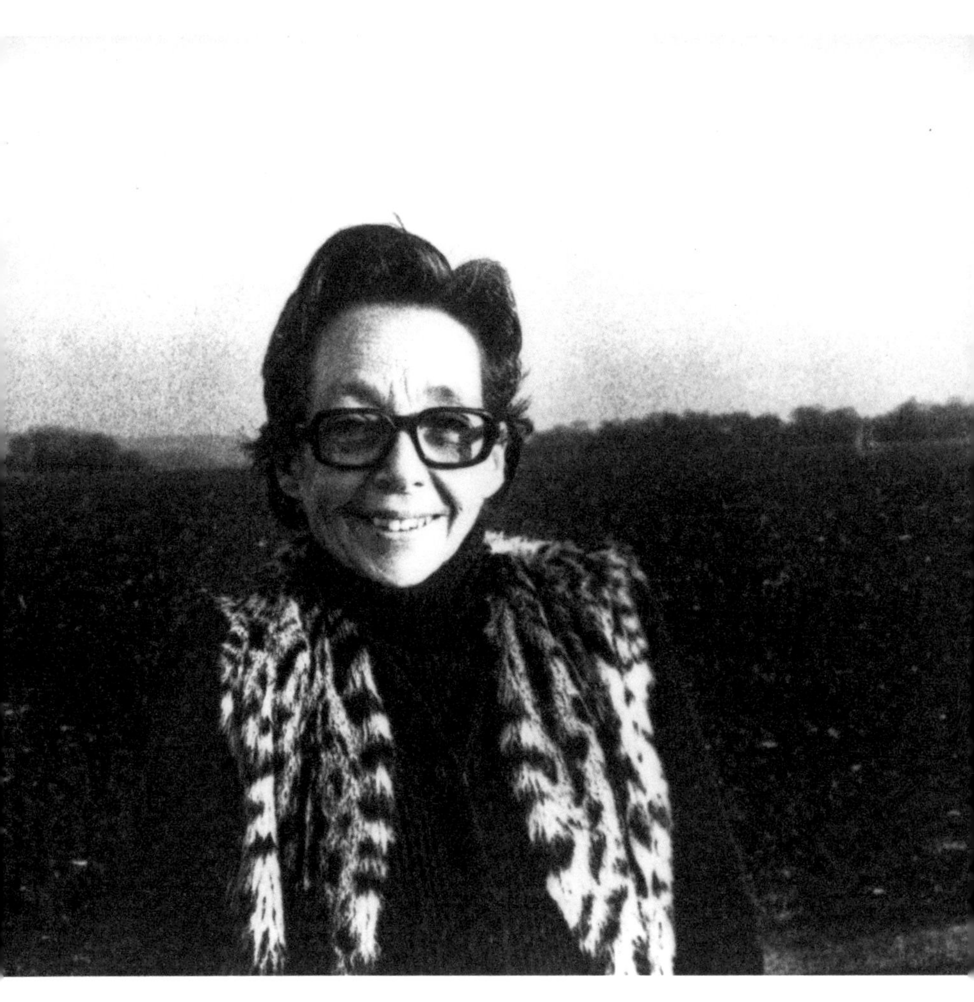

TRANSLATION OF FILM AND BOOK EXCERPTS :
La femme du Gange : p. 67, 91, 101, 103 — translation A. Strayer
India Song : p. 70, 72, 76, adapted from the film subtitles and the book *India Song*, translation Barbara Bray, New York: Grove Press, 1976.
L'Amour : p. 95, 105. Excerpts from *L'Amour*, by Marguerite Duras, translation Kazim Ali, Libby Murphy, Rochester, New York: Open Letter, 2013, p. 6, 74.

PHOTO CREDITS :
Atlas p. 58 — Fr. Barat : p. 76 — M. Duras : p. 43, 45, 47, 49, 51, 52, 54, 55, 57, 107, 112-113 — R. Gibson : p. 114-115 — J. Mascolo : p. 13 (*Nathalie Granger*) ; 66-67, 70-71, 75 (*India Song*) ; 83, 86, 92, 97 (*La femme du Gange*), 105, 109 — M. Porte : p. 8-9, 15, 19, 22, 24-25, 31, 33, 35, 38, 40-41, 80-81, 110-111 — R. Viollet : p. 63, 88-89 — M.P. Thiébaut : p. 18.